Filling Your Funnel

Building Your Business By Reaching Out To Strangers

Filling Your Funnel

Building Your Business By Reaching Out To Strangers

© 2013 by HOFFACKER ASSOCIATES LLC
West Palm Beach, Florida, USA

ISBN: 978-0-615-80751-5

Filling Your Funnel

Building Your Business By Reaching Out To Strangers

Steve Hoffacker

AICP, CAASH, CAPS, CGA, CGP, CMP, CSP, MCSP, MIRM

———

In making any sale, you can wait for interested people to come to you from various sources of marketing and promotion, or you can go out and attract potential customers yourself. Rather than waiting for people to respond to your conventional forms of advertising and marketing, a more intentional approach is to personally meet and contact people that might have an interest in what you are offering.

———

Books, Articles, Podcasts, Blogs, Webinars, Videos, And Other Content By Steve Hoffacker

To access or learn about books, eBooks, articles, blogs, commentary, podcasts, videos, webinars, and other content by Steve Hoffacker for anyone who sells products or services for a living, use the sites below.

"Hoffacker Associates" Website
http://stevehoffacker.com

Steve Hoffacker's Amazon.com Author Page
http://amazon.com/author/stevehoffacker

"Steve Hoffacker's Home Sales Insights" Blog
http://homesalesinsights.com

"Steve Hoffacker's Sales Quips" Blog
http://salesquips.com

"Steve Hoffacker's Success Quips" Blog
http://successquips.com

Steve Hoffacker and Hoffacker Associates can be found online at Facebook, Active Rain, Pinterest, Linked-In, Plaxo, Twitter, Goggle+, YouTube, Tumblr, and other business, real estate, and social sites.

Table Of Contents

Preface

I appreciate that you bought this book and that you are reading it — particularly because of the importance of attracting new opportunities for you to make sales.

Because you thought enough of yourself to want to become an even better, stronger, more productive salesperson than you are right now — regardless of how long you have been selling — you are reading this book.

It's also apparent that you are willing to take personal responsibility for generating the prospects and sales leads that it will take to sustain you in business.

In many markets, sales activity is slower and the number of people ready to make a decision may be less than what has been the case just a few years ago.

Still, regardless of what type of market conditions you may find yourself in, you can take responsibility for the amount of traffic or prospects that you get to work with.

You can take an active role and impact the amount of business you have through the contacts you generate.

This book is all about generating customers for yourself without relying on conventional advertising.

Whether you make sales by having the customer come to your location or you go to them, you can make a difference in the number of presentations you get to make.

Depending on the type of business that you have or what products and services you represent, people interested in doing business with you will hear about you through traditional advertising, such as that found in newspaper or other print publications.

They may also see your website or notice a billboard or directional sign — or use a broker or agent.

Nevertheless, these are ways of attracting customers to your location that your company generally provides.

You might also do some print or social media advertising on your own.

But have you ever wished that you could have more people interested in what you're offering and that you could be more in control of the process?

Well, there is a way to do this, and it's a way that you initiate.

Traditional advertising is fine, but you can supplement this and become much more of a factor in who shows an interest in what you have — particularly during slack or off-season times.

I don't want you to be dependent solely on sales leads and traffic that traditional advertising creates for you. I want you to be a self-generator of traffic and prospects.

Instead of wondering why you don't have more traffic, complaining about the amount of traffic you're getting, or asking your company to spend more money and run more ads, you now can do something about the amount of traffic or interest that you get.

You can do this with no direct cost to your company other than your typical telephone and postage usage.

You can make a real difference in the amount of interested people that you see.

In fact, I want you to act as though the only people that you're going to get to work with are those produced from your own efforts.

Treat the ones that your company generates for you as a bonus.

If you work with other salespeople, these are leads that you don't have to share or worry about not getting credit for — or losing to any other salesperson — because you will have produced them yourself.

I realize that this is probably a major paradigm shift — taking sole responsibility for producing your sales leads — but it's important to your survival and success.

Now, I'm talking about direct efforts — not those from social media sites or other promotions that you run that are passive.

This book talks about identifying and working with people that you have not met previously — to introduce yourself to them by phone, mail, or in-person (e-mail is not a preferred method of initial contact since people may consider it to be spam) and then to Follow-Through® with them to get them to set the appointment or get them to visit you and learn about the opportunities you are offering.

*My companion text "**Mining Your Database**: Making More Sales Through People You Already Know" is similar to this book that you are reading now except that it focuses on working with people that are not strangers to you. I recommend it to you also for generating leads and traffic.*

If your company allows you to generate customers on your own, the following pages will serve you well.

You supply the desire and the application. I'll supply the words and strategies you can use to get you started.

Use them exactly as they are (or close to it), or use them as a guide to develop your own style of contact.

It's time to take an active role in generating prospects and sales leads for yourself.

Filling Your Funnel

Building Your Business By Reaching Out To Strangers

1

Why Reach Out To Strangers?

Typical Advertising Is Passive

Many people think that the way to create interest in what they are offering is to advertise in the newspaper, magazine, or other places in print.

Recently, there has been a shift in this thinking, and print advertising has been largely replaced by advertising online or reliance on the website to generate interest and sales leads.

Generally, newspaper, magazine, and other print ads — and even online promotion or websites — are generated and paid for by your company. You may have little-to-no input on where they are inserted, how large they are, how frequent they are, how often they are updated or revised, and what their messages are.

People may also visit you because they have seen a billboard.

You might even use radio or television advertising to attract attention and create new customers.

Regardless, this advertising, promotion, and marketing that is used to generate the majority of your traffic is passive.

This doesn't make it bad. It just means that you can't control who will respond, how many people, what their needs will be, when they will want to act, and how qualified they will be to do business with you.

Conventional Marketing Is Undependable

While conventional or traditional marketing has a lot of versatility — ranging from print ads, to direct mail, radio and TV, internet, and other venues — it is undependable because it is hard to predict how many people will respond to a given message.

Often, such advertising and promotion does not produce enough leads or provide them as plentifully or consistently as you might like to manage your sales business effectively.

That's why I've written this book for you — to give you more control over the production of your sales leads.

Referrals As Sources

To be sure, positive word-of-mouth (WOM), word-of-mouth-marketing (WOMM), and referrals are a very important — and extremely economical — way of attracting interested parties to see what you are offering.

You just can't depend on the frequency or quality.

Brokers and agents — depending on what you are selling or leasing — can be important sources of sales, and reaching out to those that you haven't met or ones who have yet to contact you is an important and valuable way to expand your business.

Generating Your Own Leads

If you are relying on the results of typical or traditional marketing to generate sufficient sales leads for your business — whether your company pays for the marketing, you pay for the marketing, or each of you does some of it — you are going to be disappointed at various times.

There are going to be slack times and periods when you seem to hit a streak of unqualified or unmotivated people to talk with about your product or service.

You can be in control.

Wouldn't it be nice to know that you have the ability to supplement the traffic that your company or traditional forms of marketing are supplying for you and to take responsibility for generating your own leads?

When newspaper advertising or other conventional ways of producing traffic or sales leads just aren't enough for you, when brokers or agents aren't bringing enough people to you, when your website leads aren't as many as you would like, and even when your referrals — as great as they are to have — aren't coming at the pace you would like, you still have an option.

You can go after new leads and create them yourself.

You can choose to be intentional.

Don't be content just with the people that walk through your front door, call on the phone, or email for information.

You can go after and produce new leads by and for yourself.

Regardless of how many sales leads or traffic units you are getting from your traditional marketing efforts, you should never count on it.

Be thankful for it, but consider it as a bonus. Take the initiative for putting people in front of you.

Adopt the mindset that the only people you're going to get to make a presentation to and ultimately create a sale with are the ones you produce yourself.

Being Intentional

Being proactive or intentional is the opposite of being passive — of waiting for people to come to you. It is taking control. It is doing things on purpose.

Waiting in your office for people to come to you through conventional advertising and promotion is quite common but insufficient to be successful.

This is passive marketing. In order for you to ever meet or speak with someone generated this way, they have to receive (see or hear) your message, they have to identify with it as meeting a perceived need they have, and then they have to contact you.

You don't and can't know who they are until they take the first step and contact you. Then you can go from there.

On the other hand, proactive or intentional lead generation means empowering yourself to identify and utilize opportunities to meet people previously unknown to you (or at least people you hadn't met even if you did know who they were), introduce yourself, and begin a conversation.

By definition (at least the way I define it), intentional contact means meeting or talking with someone about what you are offering who has not visited you, may have no interest in what you are offering, or may not ever visit or contact you on their own.

Intentional contact will open many doors for you. It can lead people to you that you likely would never meet or talk to otherwise.

It's from this expanded circle of people — currently strangers to you — that you identify and meet that you can begin to generate leads and build sales.

Beginning With The Introduction

Intentional contact all starts with the *introduction*.

It means going out of your way — intentionally, proactively, and purposely — to meet someone you don't know and to introduce yourself to that person.

A proactive contact is not the time for a mini-presentation about what you are offering. Most of your discussion will come later — after you have met and talked initially.

In fact, you may not say anything about what you are offering other than the name of your company, the name of your product (if it is a well-known brand), a general description of the type of products or services you offer, and a general description of what issues you generally target. You may listen more than you talk.

You may not have much more of a substantive discussion than just introducing yourselves to each other and exchanging business cards or getting their contact information.

This will open the door for a future conversation or connection.

The primary goal in an introduction is to secure contact information from the person you have met and get permission to re-contact them.

Perhaps you will get to hear a little about their needs just in a brief conversation.

What Comes Next?

After the initial introduction with someone, you can pursue an appointment to meet with them at their office or location, your showroom or office, or a coffee shop.

When you get together again, you'll want to conduct a more thorough job of discovery about their interests or who they know that might be looking for what you offer.

Determine their interest level in what you provide and if there seems to be a possible future decision.

Nevertheless, many of the people that you meet intentionally or proactively will not have a specific need for your product themselves (or their companies) — or at least they may not initially. That's fine. It may come later, but referrals are great, too.

You are looking to develop leads — whether it's from the person you initially meet or someone that they in turn introduce to you.

It's all part of the overall plan.

They may grow into a need for the product, service, or opportunity you're offering over time or identify themselves as a candidate now for what you offer, but you also want to be introduced to people that they know who might have an interest in what you provide.

Moreover, this is not just a one-time occurrence either. They can continue to lead you to more and more new people over time — even as they and their friends are meeting additional people and expanding their networks.

This is the real value of intentional, proactive contact — being introduced or referred to other people whom you never would have met otherwise.

Meeting people and determining their needs is rewarding, and you will discover people who can use your product or service. However, there is a much greater chance that they will know people that can be referred to you.

The Concept Of Strangers

In this book, I specifically am talking about identifying people that you haven't met previously and then talking with them to determine how they might be able to use what you offer.

I want you to grow into a comfort level where you can begin approaching and talking to total strangers.

Don't be concerned initially about whether they can use what you provide or how they might be able to lead you to others. Just focus on meeting people, and the results will come.

While I'm talking about you meeting and developing conversations with strangers — that may eventually develop in relationships and even referrals — I'm not suggesting that you start just walking up to people without any pretext.

These aren't random strangers, but people that you meet during the course of your daily activities — at the gas station, the coffee shop, your office building, the market, the library, your kid's school, at lunch, at a seminar, or at the ballgame — anyplace there are people who have similar activities to you.

This will supplement the traffic and sales leads you already get, and will continue to receive, from traditional forms of advertising and promotion that your company provides. This also will be in addition to the referrals and sales leads that you can generate from talking and working with people that you already know or have met — friends, colleagues, other professionals, relatives, associates, acquaintances.

If you're not that comfortable approaching or talking to strangers, start with just eye contact and a smile. Then you can add "hello" to your smile until it becomes more natural for you. Before long, you'll be having actual conversations.

You'll be surprised at how many times someone next to you in a store or at a public event will strike up a conversation with you. Just be open to it.

2

Being A Traffic Generator

Desiring More Traffic

I'm counting on you being the type of professional salesperson who is not content or satisfied with just waiting for the front door to open or the phone to ring to see who has found you through a newspaper ad, directional sign, website, internet, or other forms of advertising that you or your company undertake.

These conventional forms of lead and traffic generation that you and your company provide are important, and there's absolutely nothing wrong with working with traffic or sales leads that are produced this way.

It's probably just not enough for you.

How often are there slack periods or lulls in the traffic

flow from people that you get to speak with in-person or interact with online or over the phone when you wish that you had more leads to work with or more traffic coming into your showroom, office, or sales center?

Maybe you'd like for your traffic to be more consistent or that you could do something about the frequency of new contacts — or that you had more appointments scheduled.

That's precisely why I have prepared this text for you.

You Can Make The Difference

You can be a catalyst for generating traffic and filling those void spots when traffic and sales leads produced through other, more conventional sources are not as strong or consistent as you would like it.

You can make a difference — in fact, you can make *the* difference.

You can take the initiative to go outside the boundaries of your office, showroom, or sales center to meet and talk to people who have a need for the type of product, service, solution, or opportunity you can provide.

You also can find referrals and recommendations from those people — directing you to even more people you can serve.

This is proactive, deliberate, intentional contact, and it so often is the missing ingredient in being a totally productive salesperson.

These are advanced techniques, but anyone can use them. It just takes the desire and the commitment to make it happen.

We're focusing in this book on reaching out to strangers, but I have a companion book ("**Mining Your Database:** *Making More Sales Through People You Already Know*") that gives you tips, strategies, and scenarios for working with people you already know.

Both sets of people — those who are strangers and those you already know — are important for you to identify and work with to be more in control of your traffic production and sales output.

Taking Responsibility For Your Traffic

Rather than relying on the traffic (people that visit you or contact you online or by phone) that is produced though the efforts of your company — or even your own general advertising or social media participation — you now can have a very real stake in the amount of people who visit or contact you.

You can create and generate a substantial portion of your traffic — even as much as all of it — through referrals and intentional, proactive self-generation of sales leads.

In this book, we specifically are talking about producing sales leads and traffic from perfect strangers and people you may know by sight but have never met — as well as the people that they may refer to you.

Not A Mandatory Action

No one is forcing you to produce your own sales leads, but why not do all that you can to be successful?

Just think of the advantage that you'll have over other salespeople when you become responsible for producing your own traffic and supplementing what you receive through traditional forms of traffic generation.

No longer will you have to rely just on what shows up — or fails to show up — through conventional advertising and promotion.

Remember that in this book we're talking about using a principle that few salespeople ever employ — reaching out to strangers for potential sales leads.

This is even more beneficial than using people you already know to generate traffic — the number of people you know may be limited, but the number of strangers that you can reach out and connect with is limitless.

The Power Of Being In Control

If you do nothing to change your method of traffic generation, you'll be no different from any of the other salespeople in your market or industry.

You'll all be competing for the same limited number of potential buyers in your price range or product offering that are reading the newspapers or other media, searching the web, or driving your general area looking for signs identifying businesses to contact.

However, you can be different.

You have the power to add substantially to the number of potentially interested people that you can talk to about what you offer — including both people that you already know as well as those who currently are unknown to you.

You can control the amount of sales leads that you have.

Being A Traffic Generator

If you want more traffic than you currently are working with, become a traffic generator.

The added bonus to creating your own leads is that you don't need to share them with anyone. This means greater customer loyalty and larger commission checks.

Knowing that you have the ability to generate your own traffic to supplement what you get — or fail to get — through more traditional means should be very empowering to you.

It can propel you into success while others in your marketplace are struggling or just working with the traffic that they customarily get.

Instead of settling for just your share of available buyers in your marketplace that find you on their own through the efforts of conventional advertising and marketing, you can go way beyond that to identifying and producing your own leads and traffic.

You'll still get your share of traffic from conventional marketing, but you won't need to rely on it.

You'll be so much further ahead of your competitors and colleagues through your own efforts of traffic generation that the traffic you receive though conventional advertising and marketing can just be considered a bonus.

3

Getting Started

Making A Conscious Decision

The first step in creating additional traffic for yourself is deciding that you want to have more — and that you'd like to personally do something about it.

Then you have to be willing to act.

Make the conscious decision that you would want to begin generating additional traffic beyond what appears through traditional advertising, signage, web presence, and incidental referrals.

This needs to be intentional and not just a wish or desire.

Then, you can go about accomplishing it.

You have so many resources available to you — ones that perhaps you hadn't noticed or thought about until now.

Two Approaches

You have two choices for identifying potential leads and expanding your traffic.

The first is going through people that you already know — regardless of how well — and the second is meeting and talking with people who until the moment you approach them are total strangers to you.

Then there is the spinoff that comes from both in terms of who they can introduce you to or refer to you.

This book deals specifically with the latter — meeting and talking with people that you don't already know.

My companion text focuses on working with people you already know and who know you.

Maybe some of the people that you include in your list of strangers are known to you already by sight but you've never actually met them or spoken with them. However, they might be people you're seeing and talking to for the first time.

Getting Started With Strangers

Constantly be aware of people around you and situations where you can meet people and talk with them about what you are doing.

Don't just go for the obvious.

Remember that the initial encounter with a stranger is just the introduction.

Don't attempt to go too far in the initial conversation — whether it's in-person, by phone, or through the mail.

You are not trying to make a sale (even though deep-down you might like to) on the initial contact.

You just want to open doors and pave the way for future conversations.

There Are People All Around You

There are many opportunities for you to find and meet people that you do not know: people you meet at the gas station, bank lobby, grocery store, convenience store, or home improvement store.

Ditto for getting a coffee or going to lunch or dinner.

Add to that business and professional people, other noncompeting contractors or suppliers who work in your market area, people in your office building, people who call or email for information that you never meet in person, people who visit with you that are shopping for someone else, and so many other situations — even people that you see in waiting rooms or who approach you in public and ask for directions or talk about the weather or the previous day's game.

Remember that you are just trying to meet people and not make a presentation.

If you take mass transit or fly frequently, there are people sitting or standing next to you.

If you go to a professional sporting event or your child's ballgame, PTA meeting, or Scout meeting, there are people around you.

The point is that there are numerous opportunities throughout each day where we can meet and talk with people if we are aware of those opportunities and are prepared to utilize them.

Tapping Into New Companies

Sure, it would be great to be doing business with some of the largest or most prominent accounts in your area — possibly some of the most influential decision makers. But there's a reason they are prominent. This is what I meant by looking past the obvious.

You know who they are, and so does your competition — even ones from outside your immediate marketplace. If you haven't met or spoken with people in these companies or organizations, and they don't already know about you and what you offer, you certainly need to reach out to them and make sure they are aware of you.

Extend a cordial invitation that you are open to meeting with them and discussing their business needs, but everyone else in your market will likely have this same idea. Therefore, don't rely on this turning into business.

So, what about newer companies or smaller ones that don't immediately come to mind — ones who are struggling to compete, building their market share, or needing suppliers and vendors who understand them? I'm sure they would love to have a friendly and knowledgeable contact like you that could help them.

Look for companies where you might be able to speak directly with the decision-maker.

Develop contacts in places or with people that may not be so obvious or apparent to other salespeople in your marketplace.

Be a few steps ahead of your colleagues and the competition.

The Point Of Your Initial Contact

When you call, meet, visit, or mail people that you have never met, you are not contacting them to try to get them to purchase (at that point) anything from you

— unless it comes out in the conversation. Therefore, this is not a sales presentation.

You are just going for the introduction — initially.

The reason you contact them — and nearly everyone else that you contact proactively — is to make them aware of you and for them to be able and willing to introduce and lead you to people in their circle that you can contact.

When you do contact them, they may not want to help you, but then again, they may provide tremendous support.

Regardless, it costs you absolutely nothing to approach a stranger, introduce yourself, and have a pleasant conversation with them — even if that's as far as it ever goes.

Remember you are *not* trying to make a presentation. You are just establishing a contact. *It's really just about the introduction.*

All you need to do is introduce yourself, mention what you do, find out who the other person is, and exchange business cards or contact information.

After you meet someone, you then can begin a dialog with them about what you're offering and learn if they might have a personal interest in your product, service, solution, or opportunity — or if they might know anyone interested in what you offer.

You also want them to lead you to their friends or acquaintances that can use what you provide.

The Benefits Of Working With Strangers

Everyone travels in their own circle of friends and acquaintances. You might eventually find that you know some of the same people, but you are reaching out to strangers for three main reasons.

First, you can't rely just on people you already know or who come to you through normal advertising, the internet, or incidental referrals.

You need to broaden your base, and you need to put a personal face on it.

You need to contact specific people, not just people in general that you're appealing to through advertising, promotion, and the internet.

Who knows? Some of the people you meet may have a need themselves for what you offer.

Second, you want the people you are meeting — the people who have been strangers before you reached out to them but now are your new-found acquaintances — to lead you to people that they know who might be looking for something that you offer.

Third, you are counting on creating an expanded network of visibility and word-of-mouth marketing about who you are and what you offer through the strangers you have met, their friends, and their expanded circle of family and contacts.

This potentially is a very large, almost limitless number of new leads and contacts.

Two Essentials To Have With You

Some of you may remember the old American Express ad that said *"Don't leave home without it"* — referring to their credit card.

Even if you don't remember the ad, the message can be adapted as great advice for salespeople.

Make sure that you never leave your office or home — regardless of the weather or time of day — without a pen and a few business cards.

These are two extremely important business tools.

You never know when you may need either one, or both, to pursue your business.

When you meet someone that you want to talk to again, you must have the ability to contact them — and that requires their basic contact information.

If the person you meet doesn't have a business card, take the back of one of yours and have them write down their name and their preferred telephone number and email address on it — or do it yourself.

Either way, make sure you can read the information and that you know how to contact them again.

This is why most or all of the back of your card needs to remain blank and non-glossy so you can write on it.

People Like To Help

Later in this book, you will find formats, templates, and scenarios to use in planned and spontaneous face-to-face meetings with people, proactive telephone conversations, and outreach written contact.

You can use them word-for-word as they are, or you can use them as a guide and adapt them to your own personal style.

In reaching out to people — in this case strangers or people you have not formally met or spoken with previously — remember that people want to help you if they can.

It's human nature to want to pitch in and help someone — to the extent of our resources, comfort level, and abilities.

Tap into this trait and allow people to help you.

Be Realistic About Your Outreach

Being proactive and generating your own traffic and contacts is a powerful way for you to have control over your business.

Just don't expect or count on this outreach to do more than it is capable of or designed to do. It will not, in itself, make more sales or necessarily make the sales process any easier.

However, it will provide an opportunity for you to meet people and make an introduction that will produce new leads and traffic that can result in sales.

When you begin making the effort to meet people that you have not talked to previously, two things will happen — you'll find people who are interested in working with you to buy something else for themselves or their businesses, and you'll identify those who can lead you to people who are looking for your product or service.

As you approach people, you really shouldn't be

interested in whether the conversation will focus on talking with them about their own needs or finding out about others they know — you benefit either way.

Regardless of what you discuss as you meet and connect with strangers, you'll have raised the level of awareness about what you are offering and made an intentional step toward attracting new leads.

Four Possible Outcomes

Whether you are meeting and talking with strangers or interacting with people that you already know, not everyone will have an immediate need for your products or services. Some might eventually, but that's only part of the total picture.

When you meet and approach strangers and introduce yourself to them, there are four possible outcomes — four things that can result.

First, they can refuse to help you. In fact, some may not even want to talk with you. That's OK, shake it off and move on.

Second, they can have an immediate need to talk with you about what you are offering, and you can engage and work directly with them.

Third, they may not have an immediate need for what

you provide, but they will in the future.

Fourth, they can introduce you or lead you to other people that they know whom they feel might have an interest in talking and working with you — with an immediate or future need.

This is the power of reaching out to strangers for their help.

Time To Get Started

Now, with a new understanding of how you want to use strangers to generate new leads and future sales, it's time to actually get started.

On the following pages, I present three consecutive chapters of scenarios for use in contacting people *in-person*, by *telephone*, and through the *mail*.

Add whatever techniques of your own that you like and feel free to use your own words and style, but this will get you started.

4

Meeting People Face-To-Face

The Benefits Of Meeting People

There are opportunities to meet people constantly. Many of the people that you see or meet are going to be total strangers to you at that moment. You don't know who they are — or if you do know them by sight or name, you have never spoken or been introduced.

As you shop, run errands, pick up the kids or attend events with them (if you have kids), buy gas, eat lunch, get a coffee, go to the store, go to the doctor or dentist, drop off and pick up your clothes at the cleaners, get your car serviced, live in your neighborhood, get your mail and packages, attend a block party, go to a PTA meeting, worship, eat dinner out, go places on your day off, go places with your spouse (if you're married), go biking or jogging, play golf, go to the pool or beach, visit the gym or spa, travel by plane or train, or serve on committees, you're are going to encounter people.

You likely do even more activities than this in a week's time — considerably more. The point is that there is never a shortage of people for you to meet.

It's learning to take advantage of these opportunities when you're around others to develop relationships and get their help in growing your business through the obvious networking possibilities that exist.

In some of your travels, you're going to see people that you already know or who are familiar to you by sight — even if you've never exchanged more than a glance, smile, wave, or "hello."

Most of the time, you'll likely see complete strangers. You may or may not even have eye contact with them.

Be open to the possibility of making introductions to total strangers, and then you can employ some of the contact strategies that I talk about in this book.

Expanding Your Network

The scenarios presented in this chapter represent a deliberate, intentional action by you to reach out to people you don't already know so you can identify those who have an interest in helping or working with you.

In your normal daily activities, you won't necessarily see or bump into other professionals, owners or decision-makers from companies you'd like to do business with, homeowners or consumers, or others that might be potential customers of yours. You'll have to make a special point to reach out to them.

They have the potential of helping you by using your services themselves or making them available to their employees or members, referring people to you, letting you place your business cards in their establishment, allowing you to advertise on their website or newsletter, and helping you keep up with the news and happenings in your market area.

You have the potential of helping them by promoting them, using their products or services, and referring your customers to them.

After a relationship is established, there are several opportunities for additional interaction and mutual benefit from these people and companies that are strangers right now.

Adapting To Your Own Style

This chapter presents a sample of scenarios that you can use as you contact people in-person that you want to establish a dialog with — people such as those you have seen socially or at business functions but have never actually met or spoken with them, people that you are aware of but have never approached about helping you in your business, and others that you might happen to meet casually as you conduct your daily business.

In the scenarios and scripts that follow, there are many ways of saying the same thing — depending on your personal style and the degree of formality that might be called for at the time.

You can say "*I just stopped by to introduce myself,*" or you can express a similar meaning by saying that you "*dropped by,*" "*dropped in,*" or "*decided to visit.*"

In place of saying "*introduce myself,*" you could use "*say hello,*" "*meet you,*" or "*say hello and introduce myself.*"

As for the people you are talking to or want to meet, you may not know whether it will be a man or a woman, so I have used "*he/she,*" "*his/hers*" or "*him/her*" in the scripts. Just choose the correct pronouns for the actual situation.

The same is true for people that you would like to have referred to you. They might be one person or more than one. It could be a family, a committee, or a business. Therefore, I have used the collective pronouns "*they,*" "*their,*" or "*them*" — both as a convenience and as the way that we generally talk in conversation.

In actual usage, choose the correct pronouns for the situation.

Visit To Area Businesses

Use this scenario when you decide to visit a retail store, home improvement or décor center, furniture and accessories store, pharmacy, grocery, entertainment complex, arcade, donut shop, auto dealership, tire shop, boutique, equipment rental, hair salon, quick printer, service provider, or other businesses in your market to meet the owner, proprietor, or manager — to introduce yourself, and to open the door for referrals. You want to open a dialog, discuss how they can help you, determine who they know that has an interest in buying what you offer — and you'd like to display your business cards or flyers for their patrons or possibly advertise with them in their establishment or on their website.

———

"Hello. Is <use their first name> in today (available)?"

[If you don't know the name of the person you should ask for, request the owner, proprietor, or manager.]

[You can mention that you belong to the same

organization, that you attended the same event, that you are business neighbors, or that you would like their help for a minute. Add that they might not recognize your name or remember you.]

"I'm <your name>. I represent <name of your company or product/brand name>."

"I wanted to meet him/her briefly and introduce myself. We are your neighbor at <street address, local landmark, or general area>."

NOT THERE — [The person you want is not present.] *"Do you know when he/she would have a minute for me to stop back and say hello (introduce myself)?"* [Agree on a day and time for the return visit.]

"Thanks for your time, and tell <person's name> that I'll stop by again on <day and time agreed on>. Good-bye."

NOW IS NOT A GOOD TIME — [You actually speak to the person you want, but they are unable to devote the time to you now.] *"I apologize for just dropping in like this."*

"I know that I didn't have an appointment and that this might not be a good (convenient) time for you. I'd really like to stop back by when you have a minute. I could use your help on something."

[Don't get into a discussion now of what you're looking for unless they decline to meet with you later.] *"When would it be convenient for me to come back?"*

[Wait for response. Agree on a day and time for the return visit or make the most of the situation while you're there. Conclude the meeting cordially.]

Agrees To Meet Again — *"Would you like me to come here, or would you let me buy you a cup of coffee?"*

[Wait for response about location of meeting and then confirm the location, day, and time.] *"I'll see you <specify the day> at <location>. Would you like for me to email you a reminder (confirmation)?"*

   Yes — *"Fine. I'll send you a note on <mention the specific day> to remind you of (confirm) our appointment on <day and time>."*

   "Which email address should I use?" [Obtain their preferred address and write it down.] *"See you then. Good-bye."*

   No — *"Fine. I'll plan on seeing you then <day, time, and place>. Good-bye."*

Declines To Meet Again — *"I understand how busy you must be. I apologize for just dropping in on you like this, but I wanted to meet you and introduce myself."*

"I really would like to talk to you for a minute. I can use your help." [Don't get into a discussion now of what you're looking for unless they decline to talk with you later.] *"Let me give you a call."* [Wait for response.]

Agrees to a call — [Set a convenient day and time for you to call.] *"Thanks for your time. I'll call you <day and time agreed on>. Good-bye."*

Does not agree to a call — *"I wanted to meet you and introduce myself so we'd each have a face to go with a name the next time we saw each other."*

"I dropped by not so much because I thought you might be interested in what we have to offer — although you might be." [Let him or her tell you if they are in the market for what you offer or look for body language that suggests they might be looking for the product or service you provide.]

[If they aren't a candidate for what you offer] *"I thought that a person in your position might hear of or know two or three (one or two, a couple of) people/companies who might be in the market for (what you offer or provide) that should take a look at (hear about/consider) what we have to offer."* [Wait for response.]

[If he or she volunteers a name or two, write it down and ask for a way to contact that person or persons.

Be sure to note the correct spelling and pronunciation. Get first names so you don't sound like a telemarketer or solicitor when you call them, and get permission to use the person's name that is giving you the referrals when you contact the other people.]

They have names to give you — *"That's great. I will call them to see if they have any interest in what we offer, and then I'll let you know what they had to say. Can you think of anyone else?"* [Wait for response.] *"Thanks for your help. Good-bye."*

No names to give you at this time — *"That's quite all right. If anyone does come to mind that you think should know about our product (service, opportunity, organization), please let me know."*

"In fact, let me give you some of my business cards in case you're talking to anyone that you think I should meet or talk to. If you can, let me who was interested enough to take my card or who you gave one to."

"Would it be OK if I left some of my business cards on your counter or if I came back with a small display?" [Wait for response, and accept the answer either way.] *"Thanks for your help. Good-bye."*

Is Available Now — [The person you are calling on can actually talk with you now.] *"Great. I'll make this quick."*

"I just wanted to stop by to say hello and to introduce myself. I'd like to learn a little bit more about your business and let you know who we are. Also, I could use your help." [Don't get into a discussion now of what you're looking for unless they decline to meet with you later.]

"I'd like to set up a convenient time when we could meet for a few minutes either here or maybe you'd let me buy you a cup of coffee. Which one is better for you?" [Wait for a response.]

[Agree on the location, and set a convenient time and day.] *"Thanks for your time, and I'll see you <place agreed on> on <day and time agreed on>. Would you like for me to email you a reminder (confirmation)?"* [Wait for response.]

   Yes — *"Fine. I'll send you a note on <mention the specific day> to remind you of (confirm) our appointment on <mention the day and time>."*

   "Which email address should I use?" [Obtain their preferred address and write it down.] *"See you then. Good-bye."*

   No — *"Fine. I'll plan on seeing you then <day, time, and place>. Good-bye."*

Visit To Area Professionals

Use this scenario when you decide to visit a physician, dentist, architect, consultant, appraiser, attorney, or other professionals in your market to meet the owner, principal, sole practitioner, consultant, or manager — to introduce yourself, and to open the door for referrals. You want to open a dialog, discuss how they can help you, determine who they know or have heard about that has an interest in using what you offer — and you'd like to display your business cards for their patrons.

———

"Hello. Is <use their first name> in today (available)?"

[The person you are asking for might greet you, or there might be a receptionist. Ask for the owner, principal, or manager. You can mention that you belong to the same organization, that you attended the same event, that you are business neighbors, or that you would like their help for a minute. Add that they might not recognize your name or remember you.]

"I'm <your name>. I represent <name of your company or product/brand name>. I wanted to stop by to (meet) him/her briefly and introduce myself."

"We are your neighbor at <street address, local landmark, or general area>." [Mention another way you know them or know of them if you aren't located in

close proximity to their office.]

NOT THERE — [The person you want is not present.] *"Do you know when he/she would have a minute for me to stop back and say hello (introduce myself)?"* [Agree on a day and time for the return visit.]

"Thanks for your time, and tell <person's name> that I'll stop by again on <day and time agreed on>. Good-bye."

NOW IS NOT A GOOD TIME — [You actually speak to the person you want, but they are unable to devote the time to you now.] *"I apologize for just dropping in like this."*

"I know that I didn't have an appointment and that this might not be a good (convenient) time for you. I'd really like to stop back by when you have a minute. I could use your help on something."

[Don't get into a discussion now of what you're looking for unless they decline to meet with you later.] *"When would it be convenient for me to come back?"*

[Wait for response. Agree on a day and time for the return visit or make the most of the situation while you're there.]

Agrees To Meet Again — *"Would you like me to come here, or would you let me buy you a cup of coffee?"*

[Wait for response about location of meeting and then confirm the location, day, and time.] *"I'll see you <specify the day> at <location>. Would you like for me to email you a reminder (confirmation)?"*

Yes — *"Fine. I'll send you a note on <mention the specific day> to remind you of (confirm) our appointment on <day and time>."*

"Which email address should I use?" [Obtain the preferred address and write it down.] *"See you then. Good-bye."*

No — *"Fine. I'll plan on seeing you then <day, time, and place>. Good-bye."*

Declines To Meet Again — *"I understand how busy you must be. I apologize for just dropping in on you like this, but I wanted to meet you and introduce myself."*

"I really would like to talk to you for a minute. I can use your help." [Don't get into a discussion now of what you're looking for unless they decline to talk with you later.] *"Let me give you a call."* [Wait for response.]

Agrees to a call — [Set a convenient day and time for you to call.] *"Thanks for your time. I'll call you <day and time agreed on>. Good-bye."*

Does not agree to a call — *"I wanted to meet you*

and introduce myself so we'd each have a face to go with a name the next time we saw or talked with each other."

"I dropped by to introduce myself and to make sure that you were aware of what we offer should you have a need for what we provide or know of someone else who might," or *"I dropped by not so much because I thought you might need my services — although you might."* [Let him or her tell you if they are in the market for what you provide or look for body language that suggests they might be looking for what you offer.]

"I thought that a person in your position, in addition to having a need for what we offer (rather than having a specific/immediate need for what we offer), might have heard of or know two or three (one or two, a couple of) people who might be in the market for <what you offer or provide> that should take a look at (hear about/consider) what we have to offer." [Wait for a response.]

[If he or she volunteers a name or two, write it down and ask for a way to contact that person or persons. Be sure to note the correct spelling and pronunciation. Get first names so you don't sound like a telemarketer or solicitor when you call them, and get permission to use the person's name that is giving you the referrals when you contact the other people.]

They have names to give you — *"That's great. I will call them and determine if there's any interest in what we offer, and then I'll let you know what happened. Can you think of anyone else?"* [Wait for response.] *"Thanks for your help. Good-bye."*

No names to give you at this time — *"That's quite all right. If anyone does come to mind that you think should know about what we offer, please let me know."*

"In fact, let me give you some of my business cards in case you're talking to anyone that you think I should meet or talk to. If you can, let me who was interested enough to take my card or who you gave one to."

"Would it be OK if I left some of my business cards on your counter or if I came back with a small display?" [Wait for response, and accept the answer either way.] *"Thanks for your help. Good-bye."*

Is Available Now — [The person you are calling on can actually talk with you now.] *"Great. I'll make this quick."*

"I just wanted to stop by to say hello and to introduce myself. I'd like to learn a little bit more about your business (what you do here) and let you know who we

are. Also, I could use your help."

[Don't get into a discussion now of what you're looking for unless they decline to meet with you later.] *"I'd like to set up a convenient time when we could meet for a few minutes either here or maybe you'd let me buy you a cup of coffee. Which one is better for you?"* [Wait for a response.]

[Agree on the location, and set a convenient time and day.] *"Thanks for your time, and I'll see you <place agreed on> on <day and time agreed on>. Would you like for me to email you a reminder (confirmation)?"* [Wait for response.]

Yes — *"Fine. I'll send you a note on <mention the specific day> to remind you of (confirm) our appointment on <mention the day and time>."*

"Which email address should I use?" [Obtain their preferred address and write it down.] *"See you then. Good-bye."*

No — *"Fine. I'll plan on seeing you then <day, time, and place>. Good-bye."*

Visit To Area Business Organizations

Use this scenario when you decide to visit a business organization like the Chamber of Commerce, Business

Development Board, or Convention and Tourism Bureau to meet the executive director, membership director, or key contact and introduce yourself. You want to meet and identify people who are interested in looking at, considering, or buying what you offer due to everyday needs, transfers, promotions, relocations within the area, expansions, or new businesses coming into your area. Also, you want to become a member, get involved, advertise with them, learn about sponsorships, and display your cards in their office.

———

"Hello. Is <use their first name> in today (available)?" [If you don't know the name of the person you should ask for, request the executive director. If pressed for the nature of your visit, mention that you belong to their organization or would like to, that you want to introduce yourself, or that you would like their help for a minute.]

"I'm <your name>. I represent <name of your company or product/brand name>. I wanted to talk with <name of director> for just a minute and introduce myself."

NOT THERE — [The person you want is not present.] *"Do you know when he/she would have a minute for me to stop back and say hello (introduce myself)?"* [Agree on a day and time for the return visit.]

"Thanks for your time, and tell <person's name> that

I'll stop by again on <day and time agreed on>. Good-bye."

Now Is Not A Good Time — [You actually speak to the person you want, but they are unable to devote the time to you now.] "*I apologize for just dropping in like this.*"

"*I know that I didn't have an appointment and that this might not be a good (convenient) time for you. I'd really like to stop back or give you a call (sit down with you) when you have a minute. I think we can help each other.*"

[Don't get into a discussion now of what you're looking for unless they decline to meet with you.] "*When would it be convenient for you to talk with me?*"

[Wait for response. Agree on a day and time for the return visit or call — or make the most of the situation while you're there.]

Agrees To Meet Again — "*Would you like me to come here, or would you let me buy you a cup of coffee?*"

[Wait for their response about the location of the meeting and then confirm the location, day, and time agreed upon.] "*I'll see you <specify the day> at <location>. Would you like for me to email you a reminder (confirmation)?*"

Yes — *"Fine. I'll send you a note on <mention the specific day> to remind you of (confirm) our appointment on <day and time>."*

"Which email address should I use?" [Obtain their preferred address and write it down.] *"See you then. Good-bye."*

No — *"Fine. I'll plan on seeing you then <day, time, and place>. Good-bye."*

Declines To Meet Again — *"I understand how busy you must be. I apologize for just dropping in on you like this, but I wanted to meet you and introduce myself."*

"I really would like to talk to you for a minute. I can use your help, and I think I can help you." [Don't get into a discussion now of what you're looking for unless they decline to talk with you later.] *"Let me give you a call."* [Wait for response.]

Agrees to a call — [Set a convenient day and time for you to call.] *"Thanks for your time. I'll call you <day and time agreed on>. Good-bye."*

Does not agree to a call — *"I wanted to meet you and introduce myself so we'd each have a face to go with a name the next time we saw each other."*

"I dropped by to introduce myself and to make sure

that you were aware of what we offer should you hear of someone in your organization or in your travels who might."

"I thought that a person in your position, might have heard of or know (be aware of) two or three (one or two, a couple of) people (companies) who might be in the market for (what you offer or provide) that should take a look at (hear about, consider) what we have to offer." [Wait for a response.]

[If he or she volunteers a name or two, write it down and ask for a way to contact that person or persons. Be sure to note the correct spelling and pronunciation. Get first names so you don't sound like a telemarketer or solicitor when you call them, and get permission to use the person's name that is giving you the referrals when you contact the other people.]

They have names to give you — *"That's great. I will call them and determine if there's any interest in what we offer, and then I'll let you know what happened."*

"Can you think of anyone else?" [Wait for response.] *"Thanks for your help. Good-bye."*

No names to give you at this time — *"That's quite all right. If anyone does come to mind that you*

*think should know about what we offer, please
let me know."*

*"In fact, let me give you some of my business
cards in case you're talking to anyone that you
think I should meet or talk to. If you can, let me
who was interested enough to take my card or
who you gave one to."*

IS AVAILABLE NOW — [The person you are calling on can
actually talk with you now.] *"Great. I'll make this quick."*

*"I just wanted to stop by to say hello and to introduce
myself. Also, I could use your help — and I think I can
help you."*

[Don't get into a discussion now of what you're looking
for unless they decline to meet with you later.] *"I'd like
to set up a convenient time when we could meet for a
few minutes either here or maybe you'd let me buy you
a cup of coffee. Which one is better for you?"* [Wait for
a response.]

[Agree on the location, and set a convenient time and
day.] *"Thanks for your time, and I'll see you <place
agreed on> on <day and time agreed on>. Would you
like for me to email you a reminder (confirmation)?"*
[Wait for response.]

Yes — *"Fine. I'll send you a note on <mention the*

specific day> to remind you of (confirm) our appointment on <mention the day and time>."

"Which email address should I use?" [Obtain their preferred address and write it down.] *"See you then. Good-bye."*

No — *"Fine. I'll plan on seeing you then <day, time, and place>. Good-bye."*

Visit To Expanding Area Businesses

Use this scenario when you decide to visit a local business that is expanding or hiring in your area — hospital, school board, local government, college or university, manufacturer, research and development, distribution, assembly, transportation, or other business — to meet the operations manager, human resources director (HR), relocation specialist, or key contact and introduce yourself. Some of these organizations may already have relationships with vendors or suppliers like you. If they do, try to establish yourself as well. You don't need all of their business immediately, you just want to get started. Also, you're interested in having them introduce you to people in their organization, possibly advertising with them, conducting seminars on what you offer, or displaying your cards and flyers in their office.

———

"Hello. Is <use their first name> in today (available)?"

[If you don't know the name of the person you should ask for, request the operations manager, HR director, or relocation specialist. If pressed for the nature of your visit, mention that that you want to introduce yourself, or that you would like their help for a minute.]

"I'm <your name>. I represent <name of company or product/brand name>. I wanted to talk with <name of director> for just a minute and introduce myself."

NOT THERE — [The person you want is not present.] *"Do you know when he/she would have a minute for me to stop back and say hello (introduce myself)?"* [Agree on a day and time for the return visit.]

"Thanks for your time, and tell <person's name> that I'll stop by again on <day and time agreed on>. Good-bye."

NOW IS NOT A GOOD TIME — [You actually speak to the person you want, but they are unable to devote the time to you now.] *"I apologize for just dropping in like this. I know that I didn't have an appointment and that this might not be a good (convenient) time for you. I'd really like to stop back by when you have a minute (when it's convenient). I could use your help on something."*

[Don't get into a discussion now of what you're looking for unless they decline to meet with you later.] *"When would it be convenient for me to come back?"*

[Wait for response. Agree on a day and time for the return visit or make the most of the situation while you're there.]

Agrees To Meet Again — *"Would you like me to come here, or would you let me buy you a cup of coffee?"* [Wait for response about the location of the meeting and then confirm the location, day, and time.] *"I'll see you <specify the day> at <location>. Would you like for me to email you a reminder (confirmation)?"*

> **Yes** — *"Fine. I'll send you a note on <mention the specific day> to remind you of (confirm) our appointment on <day and time>."*
>
> *"Which email address should I use?"* [Obtain their preferred address and write it down.] *"See you then. Good-bye."*
>
> **No** — *"Fine. I'll plan on seeing you then <day, time, and place>. Good-bye."*

Declines To Meet Again — *"I understand how busy you must be. I apologize for just dropping in on you like this, but I wanted to meet you and introduce myself."*

"I really would like to talk to you for a minute. I can use your help (think we can help each other)." [This

depends on whether what you are offering is intended or appropriate for use by the company or by the employees or others on an individual basis].

[Don't get into a discussion now of what you're looking for unless they decline to talk with you later.] *"Let me give you a call."* [Wait for response.]

Agrees to a call — [Set a convenient day and time for you to call.] *"Thanks for your time. I'll call you <day and time agreed on>. Good-bye."*

Does not agree to a call — *"I wanted to meet you and introduce myself so we'd each have a face to go with a name the next time we saw or spoke to each other."*

"I know that you might already be working with some other companies, but if there is an opportunity for me to talk about our solutions with you or someone else in your organization, I'd really like to do that."

[Wait for response. See if there is an opportunity to work with this person and get referrals from them.]

They Will Work With You — *"That's great. Are you the one I'll be meeting with or is there someone else in your organization I should be talking with?"* [If you need to talk with individual people about what you offer rather than the company or specific people in the company who make purchasing decisions for the organization, ask for referrals or suggestions of who they think you should meet or talk with in the company or outside.]

[Wait for response. If he or she volunteers a name or two, write it down and ask for a way to contact that person or persons. Be sure to note the correct spelling and pronunciation. Get first names so you don't sound like a telemarketer or solicitor when you call them, and get permission to use the person's name that is giving you the referrals when you contact the other people.]

"I will call them and see how I can help. Thanks for your time. Good-bye."

They Already Have A Relationship — *"That's quite all right. I understand. If there's any chance that I could help you or any of your employees (associates, friends) in the future, I'd welcome the opportunity to talk with you or them."* [Wait for response.] *"Thanks for your time. Good-bye."*

Is Available Now — [The person you are attempting to visit can actually talk with you now.] *"Great. I'll make this quick."*

"I just wanted to stop by to say hello and to introduce myself. Also, I think we could help each other." [Again,

depending on your audience and what you are offering.]

[Don't get into a discussion now of what you're looking for unless they decline to meet with you later.] *"I'd like to set up a convenient time when we could meet for a few minutes either here or maybe you'd let me buy you a cup of coffee. Which one is better for you?"* [Wait for a response.]

[Agree on the location, and set a convenient time and day.] *"Thanks for your time, and I'll see you <place agreed on> on <day and time agreed on>. Would you like for me to email you a reminder (confirmation)?"* [Wait for response.]

> **Yes** — *"Fine. I'll send you a note on <mention the specific day> to confirm (remind you of) our appointment on <mention the day and time>."*

> *"Which email address should I use?"* [Obtain their preferred address and write it down.] *"See you then. Good-bye."*

> **No** — *"Fine. I'll plan on seeing you then <day, time, and place>. Good-bye."*

Visit To New Area Businesses

Use this scenario when you decide to visit a local business that is brand new to your market — to meet the owner, manager, human resources director (HR), relocation specialist, or key contact and introduce yourself. This is a startup company or one new to your market, and will vary in size and what they produce or offer at that location. You are interested in working with them and their employees (depending on the product or service you offer). Also, you're interested in possibly advertising with them, conducting seminars, or displaying your cards and flyers in their office.

———

"Hello."

[You likely won't know the name of the person you should ask for unless you've done your homework ahead of time by calling to learn the name of the person you should speak with or determining it from their website. Otherwise, depending on the size of the company, ask for the owner, manager, or HR director. If pressed for the nature of your visit, mention that that you want to introduce yourself and welcome them to the neighborhood.]

"I'm <your name>. I represent <name of your company or product/brand name>. I wanted to meet him/her and welcome you and your company to <name of your city, town, area, or neighborhood>."

NOT THERE — [The person you want is not present.] *"Do you know when he/she would have a minute for me to stop back and say hello (introduce myself, meet him/her)?"* [Agree on a day and time for the return visit.]

"Thanks for your time, and tell <person's name> that I'll stop by again on <day and time agreed on>. Good luck here in < your city, town, or neighborhood>. Good-bye."

Now Is Not A Good Time — [You actually speak to the person you want, but they are unable to devote the time to you now.] *"I apologize for just dropping in like this."*

"I know that I didn't have an appointment and that this might not be a good (convenient) time for you. I'd really like to stop back by when you have a minute (when it's convenient) so I could hear a little bit about what you do."

"When would it be convenient for me to come back and meet with you?"

[Wait for response. Agree on a day and time for the return visit or make the most of the situation while you're there.]

Agrees To Meet Again — *"Would you like me to come here, or would you let me buy you a cup of coffee?"* [Wait for response about the location of the meeting and then confirm the location, day, and time.] *"I'll see* *you <specify the day> at <location>. Would you like for me to email you a reminder (confirmation)?"*

Yes — *"Fine. I'll send you a note on <mention the specific day> to remind you of (confirm) our appointment on <day and time>."*

"Which email address should I use?" [Obtain their preferred address and write it down.] *"See you then. Good-bye."*

No — *"Fine. I'll plan on seeing you then <day, time, and place>. Good-bye."*

Declines To Meet Again — *"I understand how busy you must be. I apologize for just dropping in on you like this, but I wanted to meet you and introduce myself — and welcome you to the neighborhood (area)."*

"Let me give you a call later. I'd like to hear more about what you do." [Wait for response.]

Agrees to a call — [Set a convenient day and time for you to call.] *"Thanks for your time. I'll call you <day and time agreed on>. Good-bye."*

Does not agree to a call — *"I wanted to meet you and introduce myself so we'd each have a face to go with a name the next time we saw or spoke to each other."*

"I know that you might already be working with some other companies in our area, but if there is an opportunity for me to talk about our solutions with you or someone else in your organization, I'd really like to do that."

[Wait for response. See if there is an opportunity to work with this person or someone else in their company and to get referrals from them.]

They Will Work With You — *"That's great. Are you the one I'll be meeting with or is there someone else in your organization I should be talking with?"*

[If you need to talk with individual people about what you offer rather than the company or specific people in the company who make purchasing decisions for the organization, ask for referrals or suggestions of who they think you should meet or talk with in the company or at other locations, including their homes.]

[Wait for response. If he or she volunteers a name or two, write it down and ask for a way to contact that person or persons. Be sure to note the correct spelling and pronunciation. Get first names so you don't sound like a telemarketer or solicitor when you call them, and get permission to use the person's name that is giving you the referrals when you contact the other people.]

"I will call them and see how I can help. Thanks for your time. Good-bye."

They Already Have A Relationship — *"That's quite all right. I understand. If there's any chance that I could help you or any of your employees (associates, friends) in the future, I'd welcome the opportunity to talk with you or them."* [Wait for response.] *"Thanks for your time. Good-bye."*

Is Available Now — [The person you are calling on can actually talk with you now.] *"Great. I'll make this quick."*

"I just wanted to stop by to say hello and to introduce myself — and welcome you to the neighborhood (area)."

"Also, I think we might be able to help each other." [Again, depending on your audience and what you are offering.]

[Don't get into a discussion now of what you're looking for unless they decline to meet with you later.] *"I'd like to set up a convenient time when we could meet for a few minutes either here or maybe you'd let me buy you a cup of coffee. Which one is better for you?"* [Wait for a response.]

[Agree on the location, and set a convenient time and day.] *"Thanks for your time, and I'll see you <place agreed on> on <day and time agreed on>. Would you* *like for me to email you a reminder (confirmation)?"* [Wait for response.]

> **Yes** — *"Fine. I'll send you a note on <mention the specific day> to confirm (remind you of) our appointment on <mention the day and time>."*
>
> *"Which email address should I use?"* [Obtain their preferred address and write it down.] *"See you then. Good-bye."*
>
> **No** — *"Fine. I'll plan on seeing you then <day, time, and place>. Good-bye."*

Visit To Area Realty Offices

As long as you are not involved in residential real estate, use this scenario when you decide to visit a realty office in your marketplace to meet the owner, manager, broker, or a particular Realtor® and introduce yourself. You may not know the name of the person to ask for, but it might be printed on the door. You want to learn about the market and create a bird-dog that will help you with referrals.

———

"Hello. Is <use their first name> in today (available)?"

[If you don't know the name of the person you should ask for, request the office manager or broker.]

"I'm <your name>. I represent <name of your company or product/brand name>. I wanted to introduce myself to <broker or Realtor®>."

"We are your neighbor at <street address, local landmark, or other description that they would recognize>."

NOT THERE — [The person you want to see is not present.] *"Do you know when he/she would have a minute (be available) for me to stop back (drop in) and say hello (introduce myself)?"* [Agree on a day and time for the return visit.]

"Thanks for your time, and tell <person's name> that I'll stop by again on <day and time agreed on>. Good-bye."

NOW IS NOT A GOOD TIME — [You actually speak to the person you want, but they are unable to devote the time to you now.] *"I apologize for just dropping in like this. I just wanted to meet you and introduce myself."*

"I'm sorry I caught you at an inconvenient (busy) time, but I want to discuss a mutually beneficial business relationship with you and I'd really like to stop back by when you have a minute."

[Don't get into a discussion now of what you're looking for unless they decline to meet with you later.] *"When would it be convenient for me to come back (stop in again, return)?"*

[Wait for response. Agree on a day and time for the return visit or make the most of the situation while you're there.]

Agrees To Meet Again — *"Would you like me to come here, or would you let me buy you a cup of coffee?"*

[Wait for response about location of meeting and then confirm the location, day, and time.] *"I'll see you <specify the day> at <location>. Would you like for me to email you a reminder (confirmation)?"*

   Yes — *"Fine. I'll send you a note on <mention the specific day> to remind you of (confirm) our appointment on <day and time>."*

   "Which email address should I use?" [Obtain their preferred address and write it down.] *"See you then. Good-bye."*

   No — *"Fine. I'll plan on seeing you then <day, time, and place>. Good-bye."*

Declines To Meet Again — *"I understand how busy you must be. I apologize for just dropping in on you like this, but I wanted to meet influential people in this area like you and introduce myself."*

"I really would like to talk to you for a minute. I think we can help each other." [Don't get into a discussion now of what you're looking for unless they decline to talk with you later.] *"Let me give you a call."* [Wait for response.]

Agrees to a call — [Set a convenient day and time for you to call.] *"Thanks for your time. I'll call you <day and time agreed on>. Good-bye."*

Does not agree to a call — *"I wanted to meet you and introduce myself so we'd each have a face to go with a name the next time we saw or spoke to each other."*

"I dropped by to talk about how we might establish a mutually beneficial business relationship." [If there seems to be some interest in what you're suggesting or mentioning, set an appointment to meet or talk more later. If there does not seem to be any interest in working with you or even hearing about your proposal, conclude your conversation and leave.] *"Good-bye. Thanks for your time"*

Is AVAILABLE NOW — [The person you are calling on can actually talk with you now.] *"Great. I'll make this quick."*

"I just wanted to stop by to say hello and to introduce myself. Also, I think we could help each other."

[Don't get into a discussion now of what you're looking

for unless they decline to meet with you later.] *"I'd like to set up a convenient time when we could meet for a few minutes either here or maybe you'd let me buy you a cup of coffee. Which one is better for you?"* [Wait for a response.]

[Agree on the location, and set a convenient time and day.] *"Thanks for your time, and I'll see you <place agreed on> on <day and time agreed on>. Would you like for me to email you a reminder?"* [Wait for response.]

> **Yes** — *"Fine. I'll send you a note on <mention the specific day> to remind you of our appointment on <mention the day and time>."*

> *"Which email address should I use?"* [Obtain their preferred address and write it down.] *"See you then. Good-bye."*

> **No** — *"Fine. I'll plan on seeing you then <day, time, and place>. Good-bye."*

Meeting New People

Use this scenario when you meet someone for the first time in public or socially — either planned or spontaneous — to introduce yourself and sustain the conversation. This is regardless of who does the approaching or who speaks the first word. This could be at the gas pump, convenience store, your child's school, PTA meeting, your child's Scout meeting or athletic event, a neighborhood block party, a sporting event, a festival, a store or retail establishment, standing in line, a restaurant or coffee shop, a bar, a seminar, mixer, party, class, or anywhere someone might be that you could have a chance meeting. After the introduction, you can identify people who are interested in buying what you offer or know people that are or might be.

―――

"Hi. I'm <your name>." [Learn their name and the correct pronunciation.] *"I'm pleased to meet you."*

[When the discussion gets around to what each of you does, exchange business cards or give them your card and make a note of their contact information.]

"We offer (provide, specialize in) <briefly describe your product, service, solutions, or opportunity without making it sound like a sales or recruiting pitch>."

"I really would like to talk to you a little more about what we offer. May I give you a call?" [Wait for response, and be prepared for either a "yes" or "no" answer.]

Agrees To A Call ― [Set a time and date or an approximate time frame for the call.] *"Nice meeting* *you and I'll call you <day and time agreed on> (in a couple of days). Good-bye."*

Does Not Agree To A Call — *"I'm glad to have met you. If you don't think you have a need for what I (we) provide, can you at least think of one or two people (anyone) who might be looking for what I (we) offer?"*

[If they volunteer a name or two, write it down and ask for a way to contact that person or persons. Be sure to note the correct spelling and pronunciation. Get first names so you don't sound like a telemarketer or solicitor, and get permission to use the person's name that is giving you the referrals when you contact the other people.]

They have names to give you — *"That's great. I will call them and see how I can help them. Can you think of anyone else?"* [Wait for response.] *"Thanks for your help. Good-bye."*

No names to give you at this time — *"That's quite all right. If anyone does come to mind that you think I should talk to, please let me know."*

"In fact, let me give you some of my business cards in case you're talking to anyone that you think I should meet or talk to. I'll check with you in a couple of weeks to see if anyone has come to mind. Thanks for your help. Good-bye."

Visit To An Advertised Opportunity

Use this scenario when you visit or attend an advertised "open house" (business or residential), exhibit, yard or garage sale, estate sale, auction, personal property sale (boat, car, truck, camper, trailer, office furniture) or similar event that you find with a directional sign, yard or "A" frame sign, direct mail, newspaper ad, radio or TV spot, general email, online notice or invitation, flags, or other messages — to meet the person hosting the event or sale and any attendees who might be present — to introduce yourself, obtain contact information, and open the door for future communication.

————

[When you meet the owner or host] *"Hello. I'm <your name>."* [Learn their name and make a mental note of it — especially their first name so you can use it in conversation. Identifying your company may not be necessary immediately or at all.]

"I saw your sign (ad, flyer, postcard, notice, email) and I thought I'd to stop by and see (take a look at) what you were offering (had for sale)." [Use the name of the specific item if only one is being offered.]

[If you called ahead of time for directions, to discuss the item for sale, or ask questions about it, you can begin the conversation by identifying yourself as the person who phoned and recalling the phone call.]

[Don't make it seem that the only reason you came was to meet them and collect their contact information. Only go if you have some knowledge or interest in what is being sold or shown, and be sure to show an interest in what they are selling or showing. Ask intelligent questions like a serious buyer would. Engage your seller in talking about what they have. Later in the conversation, you can obtain any contact information you don't already have. Be prepared to capture and note this information in the event they do not have a business card. You can hand them your business card or agree to email them your contact information to keep it softer.]

[Just go for the introduction and save the discussion about what you offer or the discovery of their needs until later. A phone call a day or two after the visit is more appropriate. If you actually purchased something, tell them how you are enjoying it. Then you can transition into small talk and business.]

[If you didn't purchase anything, thank them for showing you what they had. Explain that it was nice but not what you need or had in mind, and transition into a business discussion to learn if they can use what you offer, if they'd like to hear more about it, or if they can lead you to anyone else. Wish them good luck on finding a buyer for what they are selling.]

[As far as attendees, treat them the same as people you meet at a chance encounter, outlined in the section right before this one on pages 83-85. Just be careful not to appear that you are encroaching upon the host's opportunity for personal gain. Go primarily for the introduction. If more conversation ensues, fine. However, stop short of setting an appointment for anything other than a phone call. You don't want it to get back to the host that you were using his or her opportunity just to meet people.]

[Make sure you have something to write down the contact information of whomever you meet. You may want to skip handing your business card and just email them your contact information to keep it softer.]

Visit To Shows, Fair, And Expos

Use this scenario when you decide to visit or attend a trade show, home show, boat show, convention, conference, agricultural fair, or other type of expo or show — open to the public or not — to meet people and begin cultivating relationships that you can use later. Just go for the introductions and learning a little bit about the people you meet. They can be exhibitors, presenters, or attendees, and the events can be at held at hotels, expo or convention centers, arenas, armories, stadiums, fairgrounds, or other venues.

———

[When you walk up and meet someone staffing the booth or display] *"Hello. I'm <your name>."*

[Because of the nature of a trade show or expo, people are exhibiting so that they can meet and contact as many people as possible about their products and services. Take full advantage of it. Be sure to show some interest in what they are offering. If you're not familiar with it, ask questions. If you could possibly purchase what they offer, ask questions from that standpoint. Engage in small talk as well — depending on whether they can devote time to talking with you or they need to talk with other people. They likely will have business cards on the table. If not, it's simple enough to ask for one. This is an ideal setting for meeting people that you can talk to again after the event.]

[Primarily go for the introduction, but depending on how much time you have for conversation, you might be able to begin a discussion about what you offer or begin determining their needs. There usually is a lot of opportunity for give-and-take in these types of situations. Take advantage of it.]

[The exhibitor you're meeting may call you after the event, but you can telephone him or her as well because your agendas are different. You want to sell them your product or service, or you want them to give you referrals. They want you to purchase what they offer.]

[You don't have to pretend that you're interested in their product or service if you're not. On the other hand, if you are, that's fine. Either way, transition into talking about what you want on the post-event phone call.]

[As far as attendees at the event that you happen to meet, treat them the same as people you meet at a chance encounter, outlined on pages 83-85. Go primarily for the introduction. If more conversation ensues, fine. However, stop short of setting an appointment for anything other than a phone call. You don't want it to seem that you're just collecting business cards or that you are acting like an exhibitor.]

[Make sure you have something to write down their contact information. You may want to skip handing your business card and just email them your contact information to keep it softer and give you another reason to reach out to them after the event.]

Visit At Your Home Or Office

Use this scenario when someone visits you at your home or place of business — someone other than a potential customer — to introduce yourself to them and learn how you might be able to do business with them or to receive referrals from them. This would include salespeople hoping to earn your business, repair technicians, service personnel, delivery staff, or anyone else who comes to your premises without an appointment or because you requested their help for a different issue you have.

"Hello, <use their first name>." [Let them begin their job — the reason they called on you or why you requested their presence. Look for an opportunity to show an interest in what they're doing by asking questions or giving them a compliment.]

[If it's longer than just dropping off a package and leaving, engage them in conversation. Start off with small talk. Talk about what they do and their skill level for making it look so easy.]

[Tell them a little about what you do while making it sound conversational — like you're just sharing this with them to provide information. If there seems to be interest, make an appointment to talk with them later by phone or in person over coffee.] *"I know you're busy now and have other calls to make, but I want to discuss a mutually beneficial business relationship with you and I'd really like to give you a call or meet you for coffee when it's convenient."*

[Wait for response. Agree on a day and time for the phone call or appointment or make the most of the situation while they're there.]

Agrees To Meet Again — *"I'll see you <specify the day and time> at <location>. Would you like for me to email you a reminder (confirmation)?"*

Yes — *"Fine. I'll send you a note on <mention the*

specific day> to remind you of (confirm) our appointment on <day and time>."

"Which email address should I use?" [Obtain their preferred address and write it down.] *"See you then. Good-bye."*

No — *"Fine. I'll plan on seeing you then <day, time, and place>. Good-bye."*

Declines To Meet Again — *"I understand how busy you must be. Maybe we should just talk on the phone."*

Agrees to a call — [Set a convenient day and time for you to call.] *"Thanks. I'll call you <day and time agreed on>. Good-bye."*

Does not agree to a call — *"I want to talk about how we might establish a mutually beneficial business relationship."* [If there seems to be interest in what you're discussing, pursue setting an appointment to meet or talk more later. If there does not seem to be any interest, conclude your conversation and leave.] *"Good-bye."*

"Good meeting you. Thanks." [Reiterate the date, time, and type of the next contact if you have agreed upon one.]

[Make sure you have their correct contact information.]

5

Connecting By Telephone

The Value Of Telephone Contact

In addition to using personal introductions and interaction to reach out and meet people, the telephone provides many of the same opportunities without needing to be face-to-face with someone.

In many cases, it's even better than face-to-face encounters because you might be working with a lead provided by someone else, or you might be contacting someone that is difficult to reach in-person.

By attempting to reach out and create a relationship with someone whom you haven't met, it's trickier than approaching people you already know.

You can't just open up your Rolodex, database, or

smartphone, and begin calling people.

Still, you may have identified the names and phone numbers of business owners, managers, executives, HR directors, Realtors®, professionals, consumers, retailers, leasing agents, wholesalers, contractors, and other businesses and services in your area that you want to contact.

That's the first step. Assemble a list of names and phone numbers of people or businesses that you want to contact. In some cases, you'll only know the business name and not the name of the actual person you need to contact.

Continuously add to this list as you see billboards and company vehicles, hear radio and TV spots, read news articles, attend meetings and conferences, see print ads and location signs, connect with people on social media, and identify other sources of names for you to contact.

Constantly be open to new sources of leads.

Telephoning Can Be Efficient

You need to meet and talk with people who can help you. You're not always in a position where you can drive to their location, and letters can take days to arrive.

Emails aren't appropriate for an introduction.

Other than meeting someone face-to-face when that is convenient, telephone contact is the next most efficient to use.

Face-to-face contact isn't always possible due to travel distances and the schedules of people you want to meet with and talk to in-person, so telephone contact can actually be a more efficient use of your time to establish the initial contact and determine the next course of action.

Expanding Your Comfort Zone

This chapter focuses specifically on using the telephone (it doesn't matter whether it's a cell phone or landline) as a proactive, intentional means of contact to reach out and connect with people that are strangers to you at the moment you are calling them.

They are strangers because you have never spoken with them before or had any contact with them — other than possibly seeing them at a meeting without speaking to them or having connected with them on social media without developing that contact.

This may not be comfortable for you immediately, and you may have to grow into a comfort level.

There are parts of this strategy that just might be beyond what you're willing to do to right now. That's OK.

Proactive, intentional telephone contact is a very effective tool to use. If you're not ready for it now, it'll be here when you do decide to use it.

Using The Telephone Effectively

For those of you who are comfortable picking up the phone and reaching out to people you've never met or talked to before, I have assembled several scenarios for you to use to reach out and contact people that can help you build your business.

Some people you will be able to reach and actually speak with on the first attempt. They may even answer the phone themselves.

Some people you will need to call again.

Some you may never reach, and will just have to leave it at that.

You may choose to leave messages for some of those that you don't reach on the first attempt, but that might be as far as it goes.

In order to talk to some people, you're going to have to talk to a "screener" or their assistant first. Be prepared for this.

In some cases, you won't know the name of the person

you need to talk to so you'll have to ask for a position or ask the person who answers your call for the name of the person you should speak with there.

You can use the suggested language as I've presented it in this chapter, or you can use it as a guide to develop your own style as you telephone and reach out to people that can help you.

The people you are going to be calling with this strategy will be strangers to you at the moment you contact them — although their name or face might be familiar to you or you might have some common areas of interest.

Therefore, there could be some initial reluctance on their part to take your call, to agree to talk with you, or to want to help you.

Just keep that in mind as you make your calls, but don't let it deter you.

If you don't try these techniques, you're leaving a huge resource of potential leads untapped.

Remember that the person you initially contact might have an interest in what you offer, but more importantly, they can lead you to others.

Again, the telephone call is for the introduction, not a presentation.

Don't Hold Back

Even though you're telephoning strangers, don't use an alias or attempt to disguise who or what you are.

Don't try to block or hide the way your calling information displays on their phone or caller ID.

In fact, make some test calls to another line you have or to a family member to observe the way your information displays. This way you'll know what others are seeing.

Make sure it doesn't say anything like "private number," "blocked," "unknown number," or anything else that hints that you are trying to conceal your identity. Your calls could easily be ignored if that's the case.

Tapping Into A Willingness

People like to help you if they know what you need and feel that it's something they can do.

It's human nature to want to help someone if we feel that we can and that we won't be too inconvenienced by doing so.

You just need to ask the people you're calling for their help and make them aware of what you are looking for — and be sure to reassure them that they have the ability to help you.

Sometimes you'll wait to address this aspect until a subsequent face-to-face meeting or longer phone call.

Just The Introduction

Remember as you're calling people that you don't know or those who may not recognize your name that you are not attempting to sell anything in the phone call except a second contact.

Mostly, you are not going to be calling people at home either. The exception would be on a referral.

When you're calling other businesses, and you are not selling anything, the "no call" regulations should not be a concern. However, check with your particular state just to make sure.

"Do not call" applies to telemarketers, which you are not. You are calling a specific person — though you may not know their name until you connect with them — and you are calling strictly for an introduction. Where it goes from there depends on how the conversation develops.

Call To A Businessperson After An Introductory Letter Has Been Sent

Use this scenario to call any businessperson or professional after initially sending them a letter of introduction. This is someone you have never met, and they may not have received your letter. If that is the case, go ahead as if this was just a proactive telephone contact. Primarily you want to meet with them to determine if they have a need or interest in what you are selling or if they know anyone that has an interest in what you offer. You may have to talk with a receptionist or assistant first.

––––––

"Hello. Is <use their first name> in today (available)?"

[If asked the nature of your call, you can mention that you sent him or her a letter and wanted to make sure they received it, that you want to introduce yourself, that you'd like to see when they're available to meet with you, or that you would like their help for a minute.]

[If they try to dismiss your call by telling you to email your information or that the person you're calling is not interested in talking to any new vendors, politely conclude your call and try again later – maybe with better results. If you get the same treatment the next time – from this same person or someone else, cross this person or company from your list and move on.]

NOT THERE – [The person you are calling is not present.] *"Do you know when he/she would have a minute for me to call back? This is <your name>. I represent <name of your company or product/service>."* [Agree on a day and time for the return call.]

"Thanks for your time, and tell <person's name> that I'll call again on <day and time agreed on>. Good-bye."

Now Is Not A Good Time — [You actually speak to the person you want to contact and introduce yourself, but they are unable to devote the time to you now.] *"I know that you're busy and that you weren't expecting my call right now. Let me call back when you have a minute."* [Set up a mutually convenient time to talk again.] *"Good-bye."*

Has Just A Quick Minute Now — [You actually get to speak to the person you are calling, but they don't have much time to talk — primarily just set an appointment for the next contact.] *"Great. I'll make this quick. I recently sent you a letter introducing myself and our company (and/or product, brand name, or service)."*

"Do you remember receiving it?" [Wait for response.]

Yes, Received It — *"Great. I wanted to make sure you received it so you'd know who I was when I called to say hello (introduce myself)."*

No, Did Not Receive — *"Oh, I'm sorry. I had sent you a letter introducing me and our company (and/or product or service), so that my name would be familiar to you when I called."*

"Perhaps it will come in a few days, but I just wanted to take a moment to say hello and introduce myself and <name of your company and product or service>."

"As I mentioned in my letter (had mentioned in the letter that you didn't get), I want to set a time when I could stop by to meet with you and talk for a few minutes."

"I want to learn a little bit more about your business and let you know more about who we are. Plus, I could use your help. Which one is better for you — having me come to your office or letting me buy you a cup of coffee?" [Wait for response.]

[Agree on the place, date, and time]. *"Thanks. I look forward to seeing you on <date of the appointment> at <agreed time> at <agreed location>. Would you like for me to email you a reminder (confirmation)?"* [Wait for response.]

Yes — *"Fine. I'll send you a note on <specific day> to remind you of (confirm) our appointment on <day, time, and location>."*

"Which email address should I use?" [Obtain their preferred address and write it down.] *"I look forward to seeing (meeting) you. Good-bye."*

No — *"Fine. I'll plan on seeing you then on <mention*

the day and time> at <place>. Good-bye."

NOT INTERESTED IN MEETING — [You actually get to speak to the person you are calling, but they do not want to set aside the time to meet with you in-person.] *"That's quite all right. However, I really would like to talk to you some more. I could use your help."*

"May I give you a call in a few days when it's more convenient?" [Wait for response, and agree on a day and time if possible.]

Agrees To A Call — *"Great. Nice talking with you and I'll call you again <day and time> (in a couple of days). Good-bye."*

Does Not Agree To A Call — [Accomplish what you can on this call.] *"I thought maybe you could help me. That's the primary reason for my call. I'm looking for the person in your organization that I should talk with about what we offer, and I'm also looking for other people who might be interested in hearing about what we offer."*

[If he or she mentions someone in their company or volunteers a name or two of outside people, write it down and ask for a way to contact that person or persons. Be sure to note the correct spelling and pronunciation. Get first names so you don't sound like a telemarketer or solicitor when you call them, and get permission to use the person's name that is giving you the referrals when you contact the other people.]

They have names to give you — *"That's great. I appreciate that and will call them and see how I can help them. Can you think of anyone else?"* [Wait for response.] *"Thanks for your help. Good-bye."*

No names to give you at this time — *"That's quite all right. If you don't mind, I'll check back with you in a few weeks to see if you might be able to help me then, and we can take it from there."* [Wait for response.] *"Thanks for your time. Good-bye."*

NOT INTERESTED IN HELPING — [You actually get to speak to the person you are calling, but if there does not seem to be any interest in helping you or in talking with you again, conclude your conversation.] *"Good-bye."*

Call Of Introduction To Area Businesses And Professionals

Use this scenario to call any businessperson or professional without any advance notice of your call or any type of letter introducing you. Primarily you want to meet with them to determine their level of interest in using what you offer and also to find out who they know who has an interest in buying your product or service that they can refer to you. You may have to talk with a receptionist or assistant first.

———

[If they answer] *"Hello <use their first name or title>? This is <your name> from <name of your company and/or the name or description of your product or service>."*

[If someone else answers] *"Hello, may I speak to <use their first name or title>? This is <your name> from <name of your company>."* [Act like the person you are calling will recognize your name.]

[If pressed for the nature of your call, mention that that you want to introduce yourself, that you'd like to see when they're available to meet or talk with you, that you were referred to them (actually you were by word of mouth), that you'd like to learn more about their business, or that you would like their help for a minute.]

NOT THERE — [The person you are calling is not present and you talk to an assistant or someone else.] *"No problem. Do you know when he/she would have a minute for me to call back and introduce myself?"*

[Agree on a day and time for the return call. If they try to dismiss your call by telling you to email your information or that the person you're calling is not interested in talking to new vendors, politely conclude the call and try again later. If you get the same treatment the next time, cross this person or company off your list and move on.] *"Thanks for your time, and tell <person's name> that I'll call again on <day and time agreed on>. Good-bye."*

NOW IS NOT A GOOD TIME — [You actually speak to the person you are calling, but they are unable to devote the time to you now.] *"No problem (That's OK). I know you weren't expecting my call right now. Let me call back when you have a minute to talk with me."* [Set up a convenient time to talk again.] *"Good-bye."*

IS AVAILABLE NOW — [You actually get to speak to the person you want to talk with.] *"Great. I'll make this quick. I just wanted to call to introduce myself and our company and speak to you for a minute. We have never met, but we are your neighbor at <street address, general area, or local landmark>."*

"I'd like to learn a little bit more about your business (clientele) and let you know who we are and what we're doing."

"I'd like to stop by and meet you for a minute, or maybe you'd let me buy you a cup of coffee? Which one works better for you — having me come to your office and meet you there or letting me buy you a cup of coffee?" [Wait for response.]

[Agree on the place, date, and time.] *"Thanks. I look forward to seeing you on <date of the appointment> at*

<agreed time> at <location>."

"Would you like for me to email you a reminder (confirmation)?" [Wait for response.]

> **Yes** — *"Fine. I'll send you a note on <specific day> to remind you of (confirm) our appointment on <day and time>."*
>
> *"Which email address should I use?"* [Obtain their preferred address and write it down.] *"I look forward to seeing you then. Good-bye."*
>
> **No** — *"Fine. I'll plan on seeing you then on <day and time> at <place>. Good-bye."*

NOT INTERESTED IN MEETING — [You actually get to speak to the person you are calling, but they do not want to set aside the time to meet with you in-person.]*"That's quite all right. I realize that we've never met and that you are busy. However, I really would like to talk to you some more. I want to learn some more about your business. Perhaps I can help."*

"When would be a good time for us to spend a couple of minutes on the phone together?" [Wait for response, and agree on a day and time if possible.]

Agrees To A Call — *"Thank you. Nice talking with you and I'll call you again <day and time agreed on> (in a* *couple of days). Good-bye."*

Does Not Agree To A Call — [Accomplish what you can with them on this call.] *"If you don't think that what I'm offering can help you, let me ask you this. Who can you think of — either colleagues or people that you know — who might be interested in looking at or hearing about what I offer? I'd like to meet them or at least speak with them."*

[If he or she volunteers a name or two, write it down and ask for a way to contact that person or persons. Be sure to note the correct spelling and pronunciation. Get first names so you don't sound like a telemarketer or solicitor when you call them, and get permission to use the person's name that is giving you the referrals when you contact the other people.]

They have names to give you — *"That's great. I will call them and see how I can help. Can you think of anyone else?"* [Wait for response.] *"Thanks for your help. Good-bye."*

No names to give you at this time — *"That's quite all right. If you don't mind, I'll check back with you in a few weeks to see if your situation has changed or if you might be able to help me then, and we can take it from there."* [Wait for response.]

"Thanks for your time. Good-bye."

Not Interested In Helping — [If there does not seem to be any interest in using your product or service or in helping you identify other people, conclude your conversation.] *"Good-bye."*

Call To A Social Networking Contact

Use this scenario to call any person that you know of through social networking sites. You are calling without any type of advance notification such as email. You mainly want to talk with them — rather than set a meeting — to determine who they know who has an interest in using your product or service that they can refer to you — even if your social media contact or the people they are referring live outside your market area. Call them on their cell phone to avoid office voice mail and "screeners."

———

"Hello <use their first name>? This is <your name> from <name of your company>. I saw your profile on <name of networking site where you noticed them and where you are a member also>."

Now Is Not A Good Time — [You actually speak to the person you want and introduce yourself, but they are unable to devote the time to you now.] *"No problem. I know you weren't expecting my call right now. Let me call back when you have a minute (when it's more convenient)."* [Set up a convenient time to talk again.]

"Good-bye."

Is AVAILABLE NOW — [You actually get to speak to the person you are calling.] *"Great. I'll make this quick. If you check my profile, you'll see that I sell <name or general description of product or service> and I thought maybe you could help me identify people who might be interested in hearing about what I offer and how I could help them."*

[Listen for their general willingness to help you. If he or she mentions that they would like to help, set up another call at a mutually convenient time. If they volunteer a name or two, write it down and ask for a way to contact that person or persons. Be sure to note the correct spelling and pronunciation. Get first names so you don't sound like a telemarketer or solicitor when you call them, and get permission to use the person's name that is giving you the referrals when you contact the other people. If there seems to be no interest in helping you or establishing a professional relationship, conclude the call.] *"Thanks for taking my call. See you online. Good-bye."*

Call To Area Business Organizations

Use this scenario to call the executive director, membership director, or business development manager at a business organization like the Chamber of Commerce or Business Development Board to introduce yourself. You want to meet and identify people who are interested in using your product or service. Also, you want to become a member, get involved, advertise with them, learn about sponsorships, and display your cards in their office.

————

"Hello. Is <use their first name> in today (available)?" [If you don't know the name of the person you should ask for, request the executive director. If pressed for the nature of your call, mention that you would like to join their organization, that you want to introduce yourself, that you might like to advertise on their website, or that you would like his/her help for a minute. If you are turned over to someone else, continue your call with that person and learn if they can help you or get referred to the executive director through them.]

[The person you want to talk with is not present.] *"No problem. Do you know when he/she would have a minute (be available) for me to call back?"* [Agree on a day and time for the return call.]

"Thanks for your time, and tell <the person's name> that I'll call again on <day and time agreed on>. Good-bye."

NOW IS NOT A GOOD TIME — [You actually speak to the person you are calling and are able to introduce yourself to them, but they are unable to devote the time to you now.] *"I know you weren't expecting my call right now, and I apologize for catching you at a busy (inconvenient) time. Let me call back when you have a minute (at a more convenient time)."* [Set up a convenient time to talk again.] *"Good-bye."*

IS AVAILABLE NOW — [The person you are calling can actually talk with you now.] *"Great. I'll make this quick."*

"I just wanted to call to introduce myself and speak to you for a minute. We have never met, but we are your neighbor at <street address, general area, or local landmark>. I'd like to learn a little bit more about what you do (your clientele) and let you know who we are."

"I'd like to stop by and meet you for a minute, or maybe you'd let me buy you a cup of coffee? Which one is better for you — meeting at your office or letting me buy you a cup of coffee?" [Wait for response.]

[Agree on the place, date, and time]. *"Thanks. I look forward to seeing you on <date of the appointment> at <agreed time> at <location>. Would you like for me to email you a reminder (confirmation)?"* [Wait for response.]

Yes — *"Fine. I'll send you a note on <mention the specific day> to remind you of (confirm) our appointment on <the day and time agreed>."*

"Which email address should I use?" [Obtain their

preferred address and write it down.] *"See you then. Good-bye."*

No — *"Fine. I'll plan on seeing you then <day, time, and place agreed upon>. Good-bye."*

NOT INTERESTED IN MEETING — [You actually get to speak to the person you are calling, but they do not want to set aside any time to talk with by phone or to meet with you in-person — they just agree to talk to you now.]

"That's great." [Make sure they are aware of what you offer.] *"Are you aware of (Do you know) anyone right now that I should talk with about what we offer (our product, service, solution)? I love to be able to speak with them."* [Wait for response.]

[If he or she volunteers a name or two, write it down and ask for a way to contact that person or persons. Be sure to note the correct spelling and pronunciation. Get first names so you don't sound like a telemarketer or solicitor, and get permission to use the person's name that is giving you the referrals when you contact the other people.]

"I will call them and see how I can help them. Thanks for your help. Good-bye."

NOT INTERESTED IN HELPING — [If there does not seem to be any interest in helping you or in talking with you again, conclude your conversation.] *"Good-bye."*

Call To Expanding Area Businesses

Use this scenario to call the human resources (HR) director, relocation specialist, or key contact at local businesses that are expanding or hiring — hospital, schools, local government, college or university, manufacturer, research and development, distribution, assembly, transportation, or other business — to meet with them and introduce yourself. Some of them may already have relationships with companies that provide products or services such as you do. If they do, try to establish yourself as well. You are interested in working with them and their employees. Also, you're interested in possibly advertising with them, conducting seminars, or displaying your cards and flyers in their office. You may have to talk to an assistant or a "screener" or make more than one contact before you get the person who you need to talk with.

———

"Hello. Is <use their first name> in today (available)?"

[If pressed for the nature of your call, mention that that you want to introduce yourself, that you'd like to offer your congratulations on their success, that you'd like to see when they're available to meet with you, or that you would like their help for a minute. You may only be able to get their assistant.]

NOT THERE — [The person you are calling is not present.] *"Do you know when he/she would have a minute for me to call again?"* [Agree on a day and time for the return call. If they try to dismiss your call by telling you to email your information or that the person you're calling is not interested in talking to new vendors, politely conclude the call and try again later. If you get the same treatment the next time, cross this person or company off your list and move on.]

"Thanks for your time, and tell <person's name> that I'll call again on <day and time agreed on>. Good-bye."

NOW IS NOT A GOOD TIME — [You actually speak to the person you want and introduce yourself, but they are unable to devote the time to you now.] *"I know you're busy and that you weren't expecting my call right now. Let me call back when you have a minute."* [Set up a convenient time to talk again.] *"Good-bye."*

IS AVAILABLE NOW — [The person you are calling can actually talk with you now.] *"Great. I'll make this quick. I just wanted to call to introduce myself and speak to you for a minute. We have never met, but we are your neighbor at <street address, general area, or local landmark>. I'd like to learn a little bit more about your business (clientele) and let you know who we are."*

"I'd like to stop by and meet you for a minute, or maybe you'd let me buy you a cup of coffee? Which one

is better for you — meeting at your office or letting me buy you a cup of coffee?" [Wait for response.]

[Agree on the place, date, and time]. *"Thanks. I look forward to seeing you on <date> at <agreed time> at <location>. Would you like for me to email you a reminder (confirmation)?"* [Wait for response.]

> **Yes** — *"Fine. I'll send you a note on <mention the specific day> to remind you of (confirm) our appointment on <day, time, and location>."*
>
> *"Which email address should I use?"* [Obtain their preferred address and write it down.] *"I look forward to seeing you then. Good-bye."*
>
> **No** — *"Fine. I'll plan on seeing you then on <mention the day and time> at <place>. Good-bye."*

NOT INTERESTED IN MEETING — [You actually get to speak to the person you are calling, but they do not want to set aside the time to meet with you in-person.] *"I realize that we've never met and that you are busy. However, I really would like to talk to you some more. When would be a good (convenient) time for us to spend a couple of minutes on the phone together?"* [Wait for response, and agree on a day and time if possible.]

Agrees To A Call — *"Thank you. I'll call you again <day and time> (in a couple of days). Good-bye."*

Does Not Agree To A Call — [Accomplish what you can on this call.] "*I know that you might already have some relationships with companies who supply <name or description of your product or service, but if you're not currently working with anyone or there is an opportunity for me to be part of that referral/vendor network, I'd like to be able to help you when you need what we provide.*" [Wait for response. See if there is an opportunity to work with them or get referrals from them.]

> **They Will Work With You** — "*That's great. Is there anyone in your company right now that I should be talking with about <name or description of what you offer> — or are you aware of anyone in your circle of contacts who might be in the market for what we provide? I'd love to be able to talk with anyone that comes to mind.*" [Wait for response.]
>
> [If he or she volunteers a name or two, write it down and ask for a way to contact that person or persons. Be sure to note the correct spelling and pronunciation. Get first names so you don't sound like a telemarketer or solicitor, and get permission to use the person's name that is giving you the referrals when you contact the other people.]
>
> "*I will call them and see how I can help them and then let you know what I was able to do. Thanks for your help. Good-bye.*"

They Already Have A Relationship — "*I understand. If there's any chance that I could help you or any of your employees or important contacts in the future, I'd like the opportunity.*" [Wait for response.] "*Thanks for your help. Good-bye.*"

NOT INTERESTED IN HELPING — [You actually get to speak to the person you are calling, but they do not seem to be interested in helping you or in talking with you again. Conclude your conversation, and thank them for speaking with you.] "*Good-bye.*"

Call To New Or Relocating Businesses

Use this scenario to call the human resources director (HR), owner, manager, proprietor, or key contact for a new start-up business or one from outside your market that is relocating or expanding into your area — hospital, college or university, manufacturer, research and development, distribution, assembly, transportation, retail, wholesale, or other business or employment center (depending on your product or service) — to meet with them and introduce yourself, even if they aren't physically open yet in their new location. Some of them may already have relationships with suppliers for products or services that you offer. If they do, try to establish yourself as well. You are interested in working with them and their employees as they are being hired or relocating to or within your area (depending on what you offer). Also, you're interested in possibly advertising with them, conducting seminars, or displaying your cards and flyers in their office. You may have to talk to an assistant or a "screener" or make more than one contact before you get the person you want.

———

"Hello. Is <use their first name> in today (available)?" [If pressed for the nature of your call, mention that that you want to introduce yourself, that you'd like to see when they're available to speak or meet with you, or that you'd like to welcome them to the area. You may only be able to get their assistant, and you may need to call again.]

NOT THERE — [The person you are calling is not present.] *"Do you know when he/she would have a minute for me to call again and introduce myself?"* [Agree on a day and time for the return call. If they try to dismiss your call by telling you to email your information or that the person you're calling is not interested in talking to new vendors, politely conclude the call and try again later. If you get the same treatment the next time, cross this person or company off your list and move on.]

"Thanks for your time, and tell <person's name> that I'll call again on <day and time agreed on>. Good-bye."

NOW IS NOT A GOOD TIME — [You actually speak to the person you are calling and introduce yourself, but they are unable to devote the time to you now.] *"I know you're busy and that you weren't expecting my call right now. Let me call back when you have a minute (when it's more convenient)."* [Set up a convenient time to talk again.] *"Good-bye."*

IS AVAILABLE NOW — [The person you are calling can actually talk with you now.] *"Great. I'll make this quick. We have never met, but we will be your neighbor at <street address, general area, or local landmark>. I'd like to welcome you to our area and learn a little bit more about your business (clientele) — and let you know who we are."*

"I'd like to stop by and meet you for a minute, or maybe you'd let me buy you a cup of coffee?" [You may need to determine when they are going to be in your area if they haven't relocated yet.]

"Which one is better for you — meeting at your office [it may only be a temporary office while their site is being constructed or they still might be selecting their office location] *or letting me buy you a cup of coffee?"* [Wait for response.]

[Agree on the place, date, and time]. *"Thanks. I look forward to seeing you on <date of the appointment> at <agreed time> at <location>. Would you like for me to email you a reminder (confirmation)?"* [Wait for response.]

Yes — *"Fine. I'll send you a note on <mention the*

specific day> to remind you of (confirm) our appointment on <day, time, and location>."

"Which email address should I use?" [Obtain their preferred address and write it down.] *"I look forward to seeing you then. Good-bye."*

No — *"Fine. I'll plan on seeing you then on <mention the day and time> at <place>. Good-bye."*

NOT INTERESTED IN MEETING — [You actually get to speak to the person you are calling, but they do not want to set aside the time to meet with you in-person.] *"I realize that we've never met and that you are busy. However, I really would like to talk to you some more. When would be a good time for us to spend a couple of minutes on the phone together?"* [Wait for response, and agree on a day and time if possible.]

Agrees To A Call — *"Thank you. I'll call you again <day and time> (in a couple of days). Good-bye."*

Does Not Agree To A Call — [Accomplish what you can on this call.] *"I thought maybe you could help me. I know that you might already have some relationships with vendors or suppliers, but if you're not already working with anyone who provides what we do or there is an opportunity for me to be part of that referral network, I'd like to be able to help you when you have a need."* [Wait for response. See if there is an opportunity to work with them and get referrals from them.]

They Will Work With You — *"That's great. Is there anyone in your company right now that I should be talking with about <name or description of what you offer> — or are you aware of anyone in your circle of contacts who might be in the market for what we provide? I'd love to be able to talk with anyone that comes to mind."* [Wait for response.]

[If he or she volunteers a name or two, write it down and ask for a way to contact that person or persons. Be sure to note the correct spelling and pronunciation. Get first names so you don't sound like a telemarketer or solicitor, and get permission to use the person's name that is giving you the referrals when you contact the other people.]

"I will call them and see how I can help them and then let you know what I was able to do. Thanks for your help. Good-bye."

They Already Have A Relationship — *"I understand. If there's any chance that I could help you or any of your employees or important contacts in the future, I'd like the opportunity."* [Wait for response.]

"Thanks for your help. Good-bye."

NOT INTERESTED IN HELPING — [You actually get to speak to

the person you are calling, but they don't seem to be interested in helping or talking with you again. Conclude your conversation, and thank them for speaking with you.] *"Good-bye."*

Call To Leasing Agents

If you are not a commercial leasing agent or involved in selling or leasing residential real estate, use this scenario to call commercial brokers or apartment rental offices in your marketplace to introduce yourself, set up a meeting with the broker, manager, or leasing agent and discuss referrals and how you can help their tenants — residential or commercial, depending on what you offer. Also, you're interested in possibly advertising with them, conducting seminars, or displaying your cards and flyers in their office.

———

"Hello? Is <use their first name> in today (available)?" [Ask for the manager, broker, or leasing agent if you are unsure of a specific name to request. If asked the nature of your call, you can mention that you'd like to see about setting an appointment with them.]

NOT THERE — [The person you are calling is not present.] *"Do you know when he/she would be available for me to call back?"*

[Agree on a day and time for the return call.] *"Thanks*

for your time, and tell <person's name> that I'll call again on <day and time agreed on>. Good-bye."

NOW IS NOT A GOOD TIME — [You actually speak to the person you are calling and introduce yourself, but they are unable to devote the time to you now.] *"I'm sorry I caught you at an inconvenient (busy) time, but I want to discuss a mutually beneficial business relationship with you. Let me call back when you have a minute (when it's more convenient)."* [Set up a convenient time to talk again.] *"Good-bye."*

IS AVAILABLE NOW — [The person you are calling can actually talk with you now.] *"Great. I'll make this quick. I just wanted to call to introduce myself and speak to you for a minute. We have never met, but we are your neighbor at <street address, general area, or local landmark>. I'd like to set up a time to meet with you and discuss creating a mutually beneficial business relationship."*

"I'd like to stop by and meet you for a minute, or maybe you'd let me buy you a cup of coffee? Which one is better for you — meeting at your office or letting me buy you a cup of coffee?" [Wait for response.]

[Agree on the place, date, and time]. *"Thanks. I look forward to seeing you on <date of the appointment> at <agreed time> at <location>. Would you like for me to email you a reminder (confirmation)?"* [Wait for response.]

Yes — *"Fine. I'll send you a note on <mention the specific day> to remind you of (confirm) our appointment on <day, time, and location>."*

"Which email address should I use?" [Obtain their preferred address and write it down.] *I look forward to seeing you then. Good-bye."*

No — *"Fine. I'll plan on seeing you then on <mention the day and time> at <place>. Good-bye."*

NOT INTERESTED IN MEETING — [You actually get to speak to the person you are calling, but they do not want to set aside the time to meet with you in-person.] *"I realize that we've never met and that you are busy. However, I really would like to talk to you some more. I think we could help each other. When would be a good (convenient) time for us to spend a couple of minutes on the phone together?"* [Wait for response, and agree on a day and time if possible.]

Agrees To A Call — *"Thank you. I'll call you again <day and time> (in a couple of days). Good-bye."*

Does Not Agree To A Call — *"I thought maybe we could help each other generate business. I wanted to talk about how we might establish a mutually beneficial business relationship."*

[If there seems to be some interest on their part in working with you or hearing what you have to say, pursue setting an appointment to meet or talk more later. If there does not seem to be any interest, conclude your conversation.] *"Good-bye."*

Call To Realtors® You've Never Met

Use this scenario to call the broker or individual Realtors® in realty offices in your market area to introduce yourself and discuss creating a strategic alliance with them for referrals and for exchanging information.

————

"Hello <use the first name of the broker or Realtor®>?" [The person you're calling may answer, or there might be a receptionist or someone else in the office that will answer. If you don't know the name of the specific person you should ask for, request the broker or office manager.]

NOT THERE — [The person you want is not present.] *"Do you know when he/she would be available for me to call back?"* [If pressed for the nature of your call, mention that that you want to introduce yourself, that you'd like to see when they're available to meet or talk with you, or that you would like their help for a minute.]

[Agree on a day and time for the return call.] *"Thanks for your time, and tell <person's name> that I'll call* *again on <day and time agreed on>. Good-bye."*

Now Is Not A Good Time — [You actually speak to the person you are calling and introduce yourself, but they are unable to devote the time to you now.] *"I'm sorry now is not convenient, but I want to discuss a mutually beneficial business relationship with you. Let me call back when you have a minute."* [Set up a convenient time to talk again.] *"Good-bye."*

Is Available Now — [The person you are calling can actually talk with you now.] *"Great. I'll make this quick. I don't think we've ever met before, but I think we can help each other so I wanted to call and introduce myself."*

[In just a few words, describe what you offer and who your ideal referral is.] *"I'd like to set up a time to meet with you and discuss creating a mutually beneficial business relationship where we can refer potential customers to each other."*

"We can meet at your office, or you could let me buy you a cup of coffee. Which is better for you?" [Wait for a response.]

[Agree on the place, date, and time]. *"Thanks. I look forward to seeing you on <date of the appointment> at <agreed time> at <location>. Would you like for me to email you a reminder (confirmation)?"* [Wait for response.]

Yes — *"Fine. I'll send you a note on <the specific day> to remind you of (confirm) our appointment on <agreed day, time, and location>."*

"Which email address should I use?" [Obtain their preferred address and write it down.] *"I look forward to seeing you then. Good-bye."*

No — *"Fine. Then I'll see you on <mention the day and time> at <place>. Good-bye."*

NOT INTERESTED IN MEETING — [You actually get to speak to the person you are calling, but they do not want to set aside the time to meet with you.] *"I realize that we've never met and that you are busy. However, I'd like to discuss a mutually beneficial business relationship with you. That's why I wanted to meet with you."*

"We can do it by phone if you like. When would be a good time for us to talk for a few minutes?" [Wait for response, and agree on a day and time if possible.]

Agrees To A Call — *"Thank you. I'll call you again <day and time> (in a couple of days). Good-bye."*

Does Not Agree To A Call — [Accomplish what you can on this call.] *"I wanted to talk with you about how we might establish a mutually beneficial business relationship to refer business to each other. I think* *that I can help you, and you can possibly help me."* [If there seems to be some interest, pursue setting an appointment to meet or talk more later. If there does not seem to be any interest, conclude your conversation.] *"Good-bye."*

Call In Response To An Ad

Use this scenario to call someone that you want to meet when you see their name and phone number on an advertisement, billboard, sign, vehicle, or leave-behind to introduce yourself and your company, discuss their needs and any buying relationships they already have, invite them to look at or consider what you offer, and create a professional relationship for referrals and exchange of information.

———

"Hello <use their first name>? This is <your name> of <name of company or community>. I saw your ad (sign, billboard, message)."

Now Is Not A Good Time — [You actually speak to the person you are calling and get to introduce yourself, but they are unable to devote the time to you now.] *"I'm sorry now is not convenient (a good time), but I want to discuss a mutually beneficial business relationship with you. Let me call back when you have a minute (when it's more convenient)."* [Set up a convenient time to talk again.] *"Good-bye."*

Is Available Now — [The person you are calling can actually talk with you now.] *"Great. I'll make this quick. I don't believe we have ever met, but I noticed your sign (ad, billboard, message) at/in/on <actual location or publication> and thought we should talk."*

"I'd like to set up a time to meet with you and discuss creating a mutually beneficial business relationship where we can refer potential customers to each other." [In just a few words, describe what you offer if asked.]

"We can meet at your office, or you could let me buy you a cup of coffee. Which is better for you?" [Wait for a response.]

[Agree on the place, date, and time]. *"Thanks. I look forward to seeing you on <date of the appointment> at <agreed time> at <location>. Would you like for me to email you a reminder (confirmation)?"* [Wait for response.]

> **Yes** — *"Fine. I'll send you a note on <the specific day> to remind you of (confirm) our appointment on <agreed day, time, and location>."*
>
> *"Which email address should I use?"* [Obtain their preferred address and write it down.] *"I look forward to seeing you then. Good-bye."*
>
> **No** — *"Fine. Then I'll see you on <mention the day and time> at <place>. Good-bye."*

NOT INTERESTED IN MEETING — [You actually get to speak to the person you are calling, but they do not want to set aside the time to meet with you.] *"I realize that we've never met and that you are busy. However, I'd like to discuss a mutually beneficial business relationship with you. That's why I wanted to meet with you."*

"We can do it by phone if you like. When would be a good (convenient) time for us to talk for a few minutes?" [Wait for response, and agree on a day and time if possible.]

Agrees To A Call — *"Thank you. I'll call you again <day and time> (in a couple of days). Good-bye."*

Does Not Agree To A Call — [Accomplish what you can on this call.] *"I wanted to talk with you about how we might establish a mutually beneficial business relationship to refer business to each other. I think that I can help you, and you can possibly help me."* [If there seems to be some interest, pursue setting an appointment to meet or talk more later. If there does not seem to be any interest, conclude your conversation.] *"Good-bye."*

Call To A Solicitation

Use this scenario to call someone (not a company but a specific person for whom you have a name and phone number) who has solicited you for their business — a flyer left on your windshield, a magnet stuck to your car door, an unsolicited email, a direct mail flyer or postcard, a coupon or other mailing you received, or a voice mail message or missed call — to turn the tables on them and reach out to them to introduce yourself and find out if they might be interested in using your product or service or who they might know that you could talk with about what you offer.

———

"Hello <use their first name>? This is <your name> from <name of your company>. We have never met, but I received a flyer (email, calendar, magnet, coupon, postcard, mailing, voice mail message) from you about your business (opportunity, special offer, discount)." [Assume that this is a good time for them to talk with you since they are soliciting your business. Proceed as if they are agreeing to talk with you now unless they interrupt you and mention that now is not a good time for them to talk for even a couple of minutes.]

"While I am intrigued by your offer (if you are) *and I thank you for reaching out to me, I really wanted to call to introduce myself to you and tell you that I have an opportunity also that perhaps you could take advantage of."* *("While I am not currently in the market for <name or general description of the product or service that they are offering> I wanted to thank you for reaching out to me and also want to introduce myself to you and tell you*

that I have an opportunity as well that perhaps you could take advantage of.") [Wait for response.]

"I'd love to talk with you some more on the phone or over coffee [if they are local or nearby]. *Maybe I can help you with your business, and there's a possibility you can help me with mine."*

"Which one is better for you — to talk again or to let me buy you a cup of coffee?" [Wait for a response.]

[Agree on the place, date, and time.] *"Thanks."*

"I look forward to seeing you on <date of the appointment> at <agreed time> at <location>." **or** *"I look forward to talking with you again on <date of the appointment> at <agreed time>. I will call you then."*

"Would you like for me to email you a reminder (confirmation)?" [Wait for response.]

Yes — *"Fine. I'll send you a note on <specific day> to remind you of (confirm) our appointment on <day, time, and location>."*

"Which email address should I use?" [Obtain their email address and write it down.] *"I look forward to seeing (talking with) you then. Good-bye."*

No — *"Fine. Then I'll see you (talk with you again) on*

<day and time> at <place>. Good-bye."

NO INTEREST IN HELPING — *"That's all right. I appreciate you taking a couple of minutes to talk with me. Good luck on your business. If I can help you in any other way, please call me."*

Call With A Solicitation

Use this scenario when someone calls you to discuss an opportunity with you that you did not request or expect — to turn the tables on them and reach out to them to introduce yourself and find out if they might be interested in using your product or service or who they might know that you could talk with about what you provide.

———

[After they introduce themselves and mention why they are calling, ask for their name and write it down. Note the correct spelling. They won't be expecting this and it will throw them off their script or pitch. Then you can take control of the conversation.]

"I am so glad you called although I really wasn't expecting to hear from you. While I am intrigued by your offer (if you are), *you should know that I have an opportunity, too, that perhaps you could take advantage of (might be interested in)." ("I am so glad you called, and while I am not currently in the market for <name or general*

description of the product or service that they are offering> thanks for reaching out to me, and I also want tell you that I have an opportunity as well that perhaps you could take advantage of (might be interested in.") [Wait for response. They may hang up at this point because you will have gained the upper hand in the conversation. They might pursue it with you though.]

"I'd love to talk with you some more on the phone when I'm not so busy. Maybe I can help you with your business, and there's a possibility you can help me with mine."

"What is a good time and day for us to talk again — during the day, or is evening better?" [Wait for a response and agree on the date and time — if the caller hasn't decided to end the call.] "Thanks."

"I look forward to talking with you again on <date of the appointment> at <agreed time>. I will call you then."

"Would you like for me to email you a reminder (confirmation)?" [Wait for response.]

   Yes — "Fine. I'll send you a note on <specific day> to remind you of (confirm) our appointment on <day and time>."

   "Which email address should I use?" [Obtain their email address and write it down.] "I look forward to talking with you then. Good-bye."

No — *"Fine. Then I'll talk with you again on <day and time>. Good-bye."*

NO INTEREST IN HELPING — *"That's all right. I appreciate you taking a couple of minutes to talk with me. Good luck on your business. If I can help you in any other way, please call me."*

Leaving A Voice Mail Message

Use this scenario whenever you attempt to contact someone by phone to introduce yourself or your company and you get their voice mail or an answering machine (whether it's their landline or cell phone doesn't matter). Just leave the following message — and only on the initial call. Remember that the reason for the call is the introduction, but it is polite to leave the message. Don't expect a return call.

———

"Hi <use their first name>, this is <your name>. I don't think we've ever met, but I'm with <name of your company>."

"I was calling to introduce myself to you. I know of you through <mention the specific club, organization, or activity that you have in common, such as chamber of commerce, church, Little League, Rotary Club, PTA, civic group, association, committees you serve on, etc.>." ("We are your neighbor at <street address,

general area, or local landmark>.") [You can also mention a friend, homeowner, or associate who recommended that you contact this person.]

"I'm sorry to have called when you weren't available. I'll try again another time, but my number here is <telephone number>. I'd like to set up a convenient time when you have a couple of minutes when I could stop by and meet you, or perhaps you'd let me buy you a cup of coffee. Thank you. Good-bye."

[This should not appear to be totally unsolicited or a sales call. It should sound like the outreach call that it is. You may try calling again, but do not leave any more messages if you do not reach the person you're calling.]

[If you get a voice mail prompt on subsequent calls, hang up before the "beep" on their voice messaging system starts the recording. Don't worry about your number showing up on the "caller ID." If they call back because they see that they have missed a call and don't recognize the number, you'll get to speak with them and introduce yourself at that time — the objective for calling them in the first place.]

Leaving A Message With An Assistant

Use this scenario whenever you attempt to contact someone by phone to introduce yourself and you get their assistant (not a "screener" or receptionist unless they happen to be their personal assistant) rather than a voice mail or an answering machine. Just leave the following message — and only on the initial call. Remember that the reason for the call is the introduction. Don't provide a lot of details and don't expect a return call. It should sound like there is a real purpose to your call and not just a random unsolicited call without any foundation.

———

[After you are told that the person you are requesting is unavailable and you are invited to leave a message.] *"I'm with <name of your company> and the reason for my call is to introduce myself and our company and to discuss a way I think we could help each other. I know of him/her through <mention the specific club or organization that you have in common, such as the chamber of commerce, church, Rotary Club, PTA, Little League, Scouts, other youth activities, etc.>."* ("A *mutual friend recommended that I contact him/her.") ("We are your neighbor at <street address, general area, or local landmark>.")*

"I'll try again another time to reach him/her. Do you know when he/she might be available?" [Wait for response and agree on a day and time to call again.] *"Thank you. Good-bye."*

[Do not leave your phone number or a more detailed message since it is unlikely you will get a return call.

After all, the person you are calling does not know you. Insist that you'll try again later. Scratch this person from your list if you think you're going to encounter similar results on subsequent calls.]

[You may try calling again, but do not leave a second message — just your name. If the receptionist or assistant begins to recognize your voice, it's time to stop calling because it's clear you're not going to be allowed to speak to the person you are calling or that this person is so hard to reach that your time will be spent better contacting other people.]

Call Back From A Message

While it is highly unlikely that you will ever get a call back from a voice mail message you leave for someone you are attempting to create an introduction and potential relationship with, it's possible that their assistant will call you for more information — whether or not you originally spoke to the assistant. Treat this opportunity the same as your original call and make the most of securing the introduction and opening the door for future discussions.

———

[After the person calling you identifies themself as the person you were calling or the assistant to that person and they ask for more information about the nature of your call and your business, you can begin your explanation.] *"As I mentioned in my voice message, I'm with <name of your company> and I was calling to introduce myself and our company and to discuss a way I think we could help each other. I know of him/her/you through <mention the specific club or organization that you have in common, such as the chamber of commerce, church, Rotary Club, PTA, Little League, Scouts, other youth activities, etc.>."* ("A mutual friend recommended that I contact him/her/you.") ("We are your neighbor at <street address, general area, or local landmark>.")

"When would be a good (convenient) time for us (he/she and I) to talk for a few minutes?" [Wait for response, and agree on a day and time if possible.]

Agrees To A Call — *"Thank you. I'll call you (him/her) again <day and time> (in a couple of days). Good-bye."*

Does Not Agree To A Call — [Accomplish what you can on this call.] *"I wanted to talk with you (him/her) about how we might establish a mutually beneficial business relationship to refer business to each other. I think that I can help you (your company), and you can possibly help me."* [If there seems to be some interest, pursue setting an appointment to meet or talk more later. If there does not seem to be any interest, conclude your conversation.] *"Good-bye."*

6

Approaching People In Writing

The Power Of Letters

To reach out to strangers, face-to-face and telephone introductions are very useful — and they are effective in many situations.

However, sometimes it's going to take a written message to make a connection or at least attempt to connect with someone — especially someone who does not know you, possibly has never heard of you or your company, probably has not planned on hearing from you, and likely didn't know that you wanted their help or business.

Sometimes, writing is the method of choice. Nevertheless, written communication isn't always quicker or as efficient as talking to someone in-person or by telephone, but in working with people you have never met, the written word can establish credibility and a sense of formality more effectively than the other methods.

It's important to have a strategy that enables you to use all three means of contact — in-person, written, and telephone.

A More Formal Approach

When working with people who are strangers to you at the time of writing — even though you might know them by sight or their name is familiar to you — stay away from the email approach.

While that can work for people you know, when you are introducing yourself to strangers or business people you have not met, an informal approach is not acceptable.

Your written introduction needs to set a business tone, and it needs to be a typed (computer generated) letter unless you choose to use a high-quality, commercially purchased congratulations card or notecard.

Emails just are not appropriate for an initial contact with someone you do not know, and they should be avoided for this reason.

It's unlikely an unsolicited email would even be seen.

When you are sending a letter of introduction, you can also include your business card, tri-folds, reprints, financing rate cards, or other information if you feel they enhance your message for the person you are contacting.

However, try to keep the initial contact brief and on-point. Save most of the collaterals until subsequent contacts.

A Reasonable First Step

In many cases, written contact is the easiest proactive or intentional contact because it doesn't require you to go anywhere or speak to anyone.

There is nothing to prepare except the name and address of the person you are contacting.

However, please make sure you do have a specific, full name of the person you want to contact.

Addressing a letter to "Mr. Jones" when that's all the information you have, or to "Our Neighbor at ...," or to "Purchasing Manager" or similar title does not accomplish the connection and introduction you are attempting to achieve.

Even though you have never met this person, you must know their name and approach them as a business equal.

Reaching outside your comfort zone shouldn't be an issue. You have plenty of time to think of what to say before sending your letter.

Also, contacting someone in writing does not depend on them being available at the exact same time that you are. No appointments are necessary, and there are no receptionists or "screeners" to go through.

After your initial written contact, then you can follow with a phone call or email.

Letters Require Less Effort

Another nice aspect of written contact is that is can be essentially the same message for everyone that you want to contact in a particular group of occupations or businesses — or homeowners or consumers if that is the focus of your product or service.

In addition, no one will be answering back so there are no planned answers or responses to prepare or rehearse in advance — either in writing or verbally.

Without the physical trip to their location or calling and attempting to reach them on the phone, written contact requires less effort on your part to be intentional.

The drawback is that you won't know if your letter or

card that you sent has been received and read — and what the person receiving the letter or card might think about you contacting them — without an additional step by you.

In this chapter, I've assembled some examples of letters and a few cards — but no emails — that you can use as you contact people that you want to reach out to proactively and intentionally.

You will know some of the people you are reaching out to by name or appearance — from having seen them in the community or at events you've attended. However, others will not be familiar to you at all.

Letters Are Only One Approach

Remember that the reason you are using the letter, or in a few cases a card, is to communicate when a personal approach is not practical or necessary.

This does not take the place of actually speaking to someone. It is just an alternate first step in contacting someone that you don't know.

Use these suggested letters and cards exactly as they are or modify them for your personal writing style.

Do not attempt to have the letters do more than they are designed to do.

They are for introductions only. You can enclose some information about your company and what services or products you offer if you feel it will help with the introduction, but keep it simple and straightforward.

Your letters should not have a strong sales message.

You will still have to speak to people on the phone or in-person to show them how you can help them with what you offer or to get the referrals from them that you are seeking.

Your Signature Block

In the interest of keeping the following examples of letters as short as possible — showing just the salutation and main body of the letter — the following information (even if you already have mentioned it elsewhere in the body of the letter, such as your phone number, email address, or website) should be added after the text of each message as a way of closing the letter:

> *Sincerely,*
> <space>
> *<Company name, with division or product group, if applicable>*
> <space>
> *<Your signature>*
> <space>
> *<Your name — as you want your customers to call*

you — plus any professional designations you use>
<Your position or title>
<Your direct office phone line or extension>
<Your fax number>
<Your cell phone number>
<Your email address>
<Your company website address>
<Your company blog address>
<space>
<Your company "tagline">
<space>
<Any attachments or enclosures>

For handwritten notes only, just sign them legibly in your own hand — use your first and last name — and omit listing all the other contact information. Enclose a business card to supply the other contact information — even if some of it is printed elsewhere on the card.

The Inside Address

Depending on who is the subject of your letter and whether you are sending it to them at their office or residence, you would use some or all of the following for each letter (except for notes), plus the *<Date>* which would appear at the top before the inside address:

<Name, including any professional designations> or
<Names, if a couple and being sent to their home>
<Title or Position, if applicable>

*<**Name of Business**, if sent to the business>*
*<**Business Address**, including department, suite number, floor, or building, if sent to the business>*
*<**Home Address**, including apartment number, if sent to the residence>*
*<**City, State, Zip**>*

Letter To People In The News

Use this letter to contact someone because of an article about them you saw online or in your local newspaper —or even news that you heard on TV. Only do this if you know their first and last name and can get a mailing address for them. A "Dear Mr. Johnson" or "Dear Award Winner" just isn't going to work. In addition to introducing yourself and your company and/or product, service, or opportunity, your letter acknowledges and congratulates their achievement, and it opens the door for a potential discussion with them about what you provide or offer and possible referrals they can furnish.

———

Dear <name of person in the news>,

Congratulations on being named (honored, recognized) as <position, accomplishment, achievement, promotion, award, honor, designation, or office>.

Although we have never met, I hope you will accept my

sincere best wishes on this honor (achievement).

[If you or a family member have received such an award or recognition as well, you can mention it — but only as a way of underscoring their achievement and not for shifting the spotlight to you.]

I would like to meet you, if only by phone, and find out if there's any way we can help each other. You can learn more about who we are and what we provide at <website address>.

All of us here at <name of your company and/or brand or product group> join in applauding (celebrating) your accomplishment (award, achievement, honor).

Handwritten Note To People In The News

Use this handwritten note to contact someone because of an article about them you saw online or in your local newspaper — or even news that you heard on TV. Only do this if you know their complete first (not just their initials) and last name and their mailing address. In addition to introducing yourself and your company and/or brand or product, this less formal, more personal note acknowledges and congratulates their achievement, and it opens the door for a potential discussion with them about what you provide or offer and referrals they might be able to furnish.

———

<Name of person in the news>,

Congratulations on being named (honored, recognized) as <position, achievement, award, honor, or designation>.

Although we have never met, I hope you will accept my sincere best wishes on this honor (achievement, promotion, award, position, designation, or office).

[If you or a family member have received such an award or recognition as well, you can mention it — but only as a way of underscoring their achievement and not for shifting the spotlight to you.]

I would like to meet you, if only by phone, and find out if there's any way we can help each other. You can learn more about us at <website address>.

All of us here at <name of your company and/or brand or product group> join in applauding (celebrating) your accomplishment (award, achievement, honor).

Handwritten Greeting Card Note
To People In The News

Create this handwritten note in the blank space above the fold or on the left side of the fold on a commercial greeting card to contact someone proactively because of an article about them you saw online or in your local newspaper. Only do this if you know their first (not just their initials) and last name and can get a mailing address for them. Don't write over the printed message with your note since you are not a friend and that is a more personal way of writing a message. Besides introducing yourself and mentioning your company/brand or product or service, your note acknowledges and congratulates them for their achievement. The rest of your message about wanting to meet them and discuss their needs can be later. Your note in this format should be brief.

<Name of person in the news>,

Congratulations on being named (honored) as <position, achievement, accomplishment, promotion, designation, award, position, or office)>. This is quite an honor (opportunity) and one for which you can be proud.

We have never met, but I hope you will accept my sincere congratulations and best wishes on this honor (achievement).

[If you or a family member have received such an award or recognition as well, you can mention it — but only as a way of underscoring their achievement and not for shifting the spotlight to you.]

All of us here at <name of your company or community> join in applauding (celebrating) your *accomplishment (award). I look forward to reading more news about you in the future.*

Letter To Newlyweds Or Engaged Couples

If you sell household or consumer items or provide remodeling or other at-home products or services to renters or homeowners that would be appropriate for newlyweds, use this letter to contact a couple engaged to be married or recently married because of an article about them you saw in your local newspaper. Only do this if you know the names of both the bride and groom and have a mailing address for them. Address your letter to both of them. Besides introducing yourself and your company and/or product or service, your letter congratulates them on their good news, and it opens the door for future discussions with them about what you offer.

––––––

Dear <name of newlyweds or soon-to-be>,

Congratulations on your recent (upcoming) wedding. I saw the announcement in the paper (<name of paper>) on <date of article> (Saturday, recently).

Although we have never met, I want to extend my sincere best wishes for a long and happy life together.

If you are going to be looking (shopping) for a <name or description of your product or service> in the near *future as you are establishing your new life together, I would love to talk with you about your plans and discuss the great opportunities we have here at <name of your company>.*

I can be reached at <phone number> or <email>. You can learn more about us at <website address>.

All of us here at <name of your company> join in wishing you the very best.

Handwritten Note Or Greeting Card To Newlyweds Or Engaged Couples

If you sell household or consumer items or provide remodeling or other at-home products or services to renters or homeowners that would be appropriate for newlyweds, use this to create a handwritten note or one on a commercial greeting card as a more personal way to contact a couple engaged or recently married, from an article about them you saw in your local paper. Only do this if you know the names of both the bride and groom and have a mailing address for them. Address your note to both of them. Besides introducing yourself and your company and/or product or service, your informal, personal note congratulates them on their good news, and it opens the door for discussions with them at a later date about what you offer.

———

<Name of newlyweds or soon-to-be>,

Congratulations on your recent (upcoming) wedding. I saw the article in the paper (<name of paper>) on <date of article> (Saturday, over the weekend).

Although we have never met, I want to extend my sincere best wishes for a long and happy life together.

If you are going to be looking (shopping) for (considering) a <name or description of your product or service> in the near future as you are establishing your new life together, I would love to talk with you about your plans and what we offer here at <name of your company>.

I know that you've got a lot on your minds right now, but feel free to contact me at <phone number> or <email> at your convenience. You can learn more about who we are and what we offer on our website <website address>.

All of us here at <name of your company> join in wishing you the very best.

Letter to Parents — Engagement Or Wedding Announcement

If you sell household or consumer items or provide other at-home products or services to renters or homeowners that would be appropriate for newlyweds or their parents, use this letter to contact the parent or parents of a son or daughter engaged or getting married that you saw in an article in your local paper. Only do this if you can get the names of one or both of the parents and the son or daughter plus a mailing address for them. Besides introducing you and your company, your letter congratulates them and opens the door for a potential discussion with them about their needs and what product, service, or solution you provide that will address those needs. Your letter will be addressed to the parents but may focus on the needs of the parents, the son or daughter to be married, or both.

———

Dear <name of proud parent or parents>,

Congratulations on the upcoming wedding of your son (daughter) <the son or daughter's first name>. I saw the announcement (article) in the paper (<name of paper>) on <date of article> (over the weekend).

Although we have never met, I am happy for you.

If you have been thinking of remodeling/redecorating (making changes to your home or the way you use it), I would love to discuss what we have available (what we offer, what we can provide) here at <your company>.

I can be reached at <phone number> or <email>. You

can learn more about us at <website address>.

All of us here at <name of your company> join in extending our sincere best wishes to you and your family.

Letter To Parents Of New College Student

If you sell household or consumer items or provide other at-home products or services to renters or homeowners, use this letter to contact the parent or parents of a new college student because of an article you saw in your local paper. Only do this if you know one or both of their names and the student's name plus the mailing address for them. Besides introducing you and your company, your letter acknowledges their positive news, and it opens the door for a potential discussion with them about their possible changing lifestyle, perceived needs, and what product, service, or solution you provide that will address those needs.

———

Dear <name of proud parent or parents>,

Congratulations. I just read that your son (daughter) <first name of son or daughter> will be attending <name of college or university>. You must be very proud of him/her, and understandably so.

Although we have never met, I am very happy for all

of you.

[If you or a family member attended that school, you can mention it — but only as a way of underscoring their decision and not for shifting the spotlight to you.]

If you are contemplating remodeling (making changes to your home or the way you use it), I would love to discuss (love the opportunity to talk about) your ideas with you and what we here at <your company> can provide to make them happen.

I can be reached at <phone number> or <email>. You also can learn more about us at <website address>.

All of us here at <your company> join in extending our sincere best wishes to you and your family.

Letter To Parents Of College Graduate

If you sell household or consumer items or provide other at-home products or services to renters or homeowners, use this letter to contact the parent or parents of a college graduate because of an article about them or their child in your local paper. Only do this if you know one or both of the parents' names and the student's name plus the mailing address for them. Besides introducing you and your company, your letter congratulates them on this accomplishment and opens the door for a potential discussion about their possible changing lifestyle, perceived needs, and what product, service, or solution you provide that will address those needs.

―――

Dear <name of proud parent or parents>,

Congratulations on your son's (daughter's) <first name of son or daughter> graduation from <name of university>. You must be extremely proud of his/her accomplishment, and understandably so.

Although we have never met, I want to be among the list of well-wishers celebrating your son's/daughter's success.

[If you or a family member attended that school, you can mention it — but only as a way of underscoring their decision and not for shifting the spotlight to you.]

If you are contemplating (thinking of/about) remodeling (making changes to your home or the way you use it), I would love to discuss (the opportunity to talk about) your ideas with you and what we here at <your company> can provide to make them happen.

I can be reached at <phone number> or <email>. You can learn more about us and what we offer (what we do, our products, our solutions, our services) at <website address>.

All of us here at <name of your company > join in extending our sincere best wishes on your son's (daughter's) achievement.

Letter Congratulating College Graduate

If you sell household or consumer items or provide other at-home products or services to renters or homeowners, use this letter to contact someone because of an article about them graduating from college that you saw in your local paper. Only do this if you know their name and can get a mailing address for them. Besides introducing you and your company and your product or service, your letter acknowledges their special accomplishment, congratulates them on their achievement, and it opens the door for a potential discussion with them about helping them decorate or accessorize their home or office or meet other needs they might have — if they are remaining in your area.

————

Dear <name of recent/soon-to-be graduate>,

Congratulations on your graduation (upcoming graduation) from <name of college or university>. You must be pleased with your accomplishment, as are we. Although we have never met, I want to be among the list of well-wishers who are celebrating your success.

[If you or a family member attended that same school,

department, or sorority or fraternity, or have the same degree or major field, you can mention it — but only as a way of underscoring their achievement and not for shifting the spotlight to you.]

As you are transitioning into the business world, and getting started on your professional career, I would love to meet with you and buy you a cup of coffee and get to know a little more about you.

I'd also like to learn about any plans (ideas) that you might have for decorating, remodeling, or accessorizing your home, apartment, or office where I might be able to provide some assistance in helping you evaluate what choices you have, what you might want or need, and determining a budget for what you plan on (decide on) doing.

I can be reached at <phone number> or <email>, and you can learn more about us and what we offer (what we do, our products, our solutions, our services) at <website address>.

All of us here at <your company> join in extending our sincere best wishes on your achievement.

Handwritten Greeting Card Note
To College Graduate

If you sell household or consumer items or provide other

at-home products or services to renters or homeowners, use this to create a handwritten note in the blank space above the fold or on the left side of the fold on a commercial greeting card to contact someone because of an article about them graduating from college that you saw online or in your local newspaper. Only do this if you know their first and last name and can get a mailing address for them. Don't write over the printed message with your note since you are not a friend and that is a more personal way of writing a message. Besides introducing yourself and your company, your note acknowledges their achievement and congratulates them on their accomplishment. The rest of your intended message about wanting to meet them and discuss or explore their needs and how you address them should be saved for a later time. Your note should be very brief and positive.

———

<Name of college graduate>,

Congratulations on your graduation (upcoming graduation) from <name of school>.

This is quite an achievement and one for which you can be very proud.

[If you or a family member attended that same school, department, or sorority or fraternity, or have the same degree or major field, you can mention it — but only as a way of underscoring their achievement and not for shifting the spotlight to you.]

We have never met, but I hope you will accept my sincere best wishes on this accomplishment.

I look forward to reading more about your accomplishments in the years to come.

Letter About Birth Announcement

If you sell household or consumer items or provide other at-home products or services to renters or homeowners that are appropriate for parents with a newborn, use this letter to contact those parents because of an article about them you saw in your local newspaper. Only do this if you know their complete names and can get a mailing address for them. Besides introducing you and your company, your letter congratulates them, and it opens the door for a potential future discussion with them about their changing needs and the product, service, or solution you provide. Just mention that you offer something that might help them or that they might be interested in hearing about. Save the details and the specifics for a subsequent note or phone call.

Dear <names of new parents>,

Congratulations on the birth of your son (daughter)

<son or daughter's name if known>.

I saw the announcement (article) in the paper (<name of paper>) on <date of article> (a few days ago) and wanted to share your good news with you.

Although we have never met, I join you in celebrating this happy (joyous) occasion.

If you think you might need (If you have been thinking about, If you have been considering, If you have been talking about/discussing) redecorating, remodeling, or accessorizing (making some changes to) your home or apartment and have been waiting for this blessed event (putting it off until your son/daughter was born), I would like to help you evaluate what you might need or want and help you determine a budget for what you'd like to do.

I can be reached at <phone number> or <email>, and you can learn more about us and what we offer at <website address>.

All of us at <name of your company> join in celebrating your good news.

Handwritten Note Or Greeting Card About Birth Announcement

If you sell household or consumer items or provide

other at-home products or services to renters or homeowners, use this handwritten note on the inside blank page of the commercial greeting card or insert your own note to contact new parents because of a news article about them having a baby that you saw in your local paper. Only do this if you know their complete names (preferably both parents) and can get a mailing address for them. In addition to introducing you and your company, it congratulates them in a more personal, informal way and opens the door for a potential discussion with them about using or buying the products and services you represent. However, this is not the time for a strong sales message — just sincere congratulations. Save other messages for later.

———

<Name or names of new parents>,

Congratulations on the birth of your son (daughter) <their first name if it is known>. I saw the announcement (article) in the paper (<name of paper>) on <date of article> (today, a few days ago, over the weekend).

Although we have never met, I join you in celebrating this happy (joyous) occasion.

If you have be thinking about (If you have been considering) redecorating, remodeling, or accessorizing your home or apartment to accommodate your growing family, I would like to talk with you about this later.

Meanwhile, I can be reached at <phone number> or <email>. You can learn more about who we are and what we offer at <website address>.

All of us at <name of your company> join in celebrating your good news.

Letter To Someone Transferring Or Relocating To Your Area

If you sell household or consumer items or provide other at-home products or services to renters or homeowners, use this printed letter to contact someone who is relocating or transferring into your area. Only do this if you learn their complete name and can get a mailing address for them. Besides introducing you and your company, your letter welcomes them to your area, congratulates them on their promotion, transfer, or new position, and it opens the door for a potential discussion with them about the products, services, or solutions you offer. This letter can reference what you do but should not have a strong sales message.

———

Dear <name of transferee>,

Congratulations on your promotion (transfer, relocation). I understand that you are going to be relocating (moving) to <your city or area>, and I want to be one of the first to welcome you to our area.

I know that you are looking forward to coming to a new area but that moving to a new area also presents some challenges, such as finding a new home and locating important services such as dentists, doctors, and schools [if applicable].

If I can be of any help to you (you and your family) — even if it's just pointing you in the right direction or saving you some time — please call upon me.

When you are actually situated in your new position, I'd love to have coffee with you and share stories of what we each do.

In the meantime, I can be reached at <phone number> or <email>. You can learn more about us and what we do at <website address>.

Once again, welcome to <name of city or area>. I look forward to meeting you.

Letter To Expanding Local Company

Use this letter to contact the operations manager, owner, manager, or proprietor of a local company that you are aware of that has announced plans to expand because of an article about their company you saw online or in your local newspaper — or even news that you heard on TV. Only do this if you know their name and can get a mailing address for them. Besides introducing you and your company, your letter congratulates them for that progress and their success, and it opens the door for a potential discussion with them about working with them, or even their employees if you offer consumer products, to address their needs.

———

Dear <name of company official>,

As a fellow corporate citizen of <name of your city, area, or neighborhood>, I am excited by your success and want to celebrate it with you.

Congratulations on your recent announcement to add more jobs (produce <name of product> at your <name of area> facility/plant, that you received a significant contract). That means a lot to our area as well as your company.

I am <your name>, of <name of your company>, and we are your neighbors [if you are located reasonably close to them] *located just <number of miles or and/or number of minutes> from your office (location) on <name of road, specific address, intersection, local landmark, or point of reference>.*

I'm not sure if you are aware of us or how much you

might know about our company and what we provide. (You may not be aware of us so that is another reason I am contacting you and making this introduction.)

I will call you in a few days to discuss a convenient time when we can talk or meet for a few minutes.

I look forward to learning more about your business and discussing how we might be able to help you. In the meantime, I can be reached at <phone number> or <email>.

You can learn more about us and what we offer at <website address>.

Letter To Relocating Non-Local Firm

Use this letter to contact the operations manager, owner, manager, president, vice president, proprietor, or other major decision-maker of a firm from outside your area that has announced plans to relocate to your market. You may have seen this online or in your local newspaper or even heard it on TV. You may have heard about it through some of your other sources. Only do this if you know their name and can get a mailing address for them — local or where they are now. Besides introducing you and your company, your letter congratulates them on their move, welcomes them to your area, and opens the door for a potential discussion with them about working with them, or even their employees if you offer consumer products, to address their needs.

———

Dear <name of company official>,

Congratulations on your decision to move your company to (begin operations in, open a division in, branch out into) <name of your area>. We've never met, but let me be among the first to welcome you to our area.

I know that moving to a new area presents a lot of exciting opportunities for your company and your employees, but that it also presents some challenges of getting everyone relocated and acclimated to new surroundings.

I am <your name>, of <name of your company>, and we are your neighbors [if you are located reasonably close to them] *located just <number of miles or and/or number of minutes> from your office (location) on <name of road, specific address, intersection, local landmark, or point of reference>.*

I know that you are going to be busy with the relocation for the foreseeable future, but I would welcome the opportunity just to say hello and treat you to a cup of coffee the next time you are going to be in our area.

I will call you in a few days to discuss setting a time for us to meet.

In the meantime, I can be reached at <phone number> or <email>. You can learn more about us and what we offer at <website address>.

Once again, welcome to <name of your city or area>.

Letter Of Introduction To A Specific Businessperson

Use this letter to contact someone because you know who they are by sight or name — possibly you are even members of the same organization — but you have never met them or been introduced. This letter states what the two of you have in common and serves as an introduction of you and your company. It opens the door for a potential discussion with them about doing business with them and for meeting people they can refer to you who might have an interest in what you offer. This is the preliminary step to contacting them by phone. Only do this if you know their name and can get a mailing address for them.

———

Dear <name of businessperson>,

Please allow me to introduce myself. We have never formally met, but I have seen you at the <mention the

event, group, activity, function, or location where you have seen them or know of them, even if you have not directly made eye contact with each other in the past or exchanged a "hello" — such as a business group, luncheon, seminar, large committee meeting, chamber of commerce, church, or civic group>, and I would like to meet you.

I look forward to meeting with you and learning more about your business. I'd also like to talk to you about <name of your company> and what we offer. I think we can help each other.

I will give you a call in a couple of days to see when you are available (to schedule a convenient time) to meet with me for a cup of coffee.

In the meantime, I can be reached at <phone number> or <email>. You can learn more about us and what we offer at <website address>.

Letter To Area Businesses And Professionals

Use this letter to contact area business owners, managers, and professionals to introduce you and your company and open the door for a potential discussion with them about using your product, service, solution, or opportunity or in leading you to other people they know who may have an interest in what you offer. You are going to be calling them after sending this letter of introduction. This is the first step in meeting them and developing a relationship. Only send this letter if you know their name and can get a mailing address for them.

———

Dear <first name of businessperson, if appropriate>,

I am <your name> and I'm sending you this brief note to introduce myself and my company. We are <name of your company>, your neighbors at <street address or local landmark>.

I'll get right to the point. I'd like to meet you.

I will call you in a few days to see if we can schedule a time for a cup of coffee so I can learn a little more about your business and share with you how I think I can help you.

In the meantime, I can be reached at <phone number> or <email>. You can learn more about us and what we offer at <website address>.

Letter To A Nearby Renter

If you sell household or consumer items or provide other at-home products or services specifically for renters, use this letter to contact residents of a nearby rental complex about the possibilities you offer for their comfort, safety, or enjoyment of their residence or lifestyle. Only do this if you can get their name and a mailing address for them. Your letter will introduce you and your company and open the door for a potential discussion with them about what you offer.

———

Dear <name or names of renter or renters>,

Allow me to introduce myself. I am <your name> of <name of your company>, your neighbor at <address, local landmark, or point of reference>.

I am contacting you because I think we have a product (service, solution, opportunity) that will help you, and I want to meet with you to talk about what we offer.

I can be reached at <phone number> or <email>. You can learn more about us and what we offer at <website address>.

I look forward to hearing from (meeting, talking with) you.

Letter To An Area Homeowner

If you sell household or consumer items or provide other at-home products, services, or solutions specifically for homeowners, use this letter to contact nearby homeowners in your general market area about the possibilities you offer for their comfort, safety, or enjoyment of their residence, auto, or lifestyle. Only do this if you can get their name and a mailing address for them. Your letter introduces you and your company and it opens the door for a potential discussion with them about what you offer.

———

Dear <name or names of owner or owners>,

Allow me to introduce myself. I am <your name> of <name of your company>, your neighbor at <address, local landmark, or point of reference>.

I am contacting you because I think we have a product (service, solution, opportunity) that will help you, and I want to meet with you to talk about what we offer.

I can be reached at <phone number> or <email>. You can learn more about us and what we offer at <website address>.

I look forward to hearing from you.

7

Making It Work

An Entrepreneurial Approach

As an entrepreneur, you have no customers. They don't come in the box you get when you decide to open a business or go into sales. You can't go to the office supply store and purchase them.

You're starting from scratch. You examine your options for customers — the lifeblood of your business — and determine that you have three viable choices.

Option one — you stay in your office, showroom, or sales center and greet the traffic or sales leads that are supplied through conventional means. This includes all forms of print advertising, electronic media, signage, internet, and broker or agent traffic and referrals.

Of course, you maintain post-visit Follow-Through® contact with everyone you meet according to their level of interest and ability to make a decision as you develop and cultivate those leads until a transaction is possible.

Option two — you talk to people you already know and begin developing your own sales leads. This is discussed in my companion book for lead generation: "**Mining Your Database:** *Making More Sales Through People You Already Know.*"

Option three — you reach out to people you don't know or haven't met. You involve strangers in your business and begin building sales and referrals with their help.

You Aren't Owed Success

This is what we've been discussing and preparing you for in this book, and this is where you have the greatest freedom and potential to make it really big.

You recognize that as a business builder you aren't owed anything except the opportunity for success, so you take it upon yourself to generate your own sales leads that can hasten your success.

This is what's going to give you the additional edge and earning power over other salespeople in your market.

Most salespeople are content to work with the traffic or sales leads that walk through their front door or are otherwise generated by their company.

This is unpredictable and shortsighted. It is not a dependable or consistent form of lead generation.

Empowering Yourself For Success

With the knowledge that you can produce your own sales leads and make traffic appear that you have generated, you can be an outstanding success.

This is powerful.

By reaching out to people that you don't know, you're going to be adding an element to your sales program that most other salespeople are missing — regardless of their product, service, price point, target audience, or territory.

There is no effective limit to the number of sales leads that you can generate this way. You have the power to be as successful as you want.

Generating your own leads — particularly by reaching out to contact and work with people you don't know — can make the difference in your success.

It will enable you to make a statement and thrive in your marketplace.

You will be eliminating the total dependence on conventional marketing and advertising, and any help your company might provide, as the source of your traffic and sales leads.

Empowerment Is Taken

Empowering yourself to begin generating your own leads — by doing things for yourself and working with either friends or strangers — is not something you have to be invited to do or given permission to start.

Empowerment is taken. It is not given. Don't wait for it to be offered.

Just decide that generating your own leads is something that makes sense for you to do — even if you're not totally comfortable with the idea of meeting strangers and developing them into sales leads or referrals.

Then, you will have empowered yourself to begin expanding your business and taking responsibility for producing the most crucial element of your sales program — your future customers.

Going Beyond The Obvious

While talking to people that you already know and asking them for referrals will net you many additional opportunities to make sales, other ambitious salespeople in your market or type of business can do the same thing with their circle of contacts.

They may not be as comprehensive as you are or able to identify the variety of people that you can contact, but starting with referrals from existing satisfied customers and from family and friends are common ways to generate more traffic.

Nevertheless, when you use some of the scenarios and strategies that are in my companion lead generation book, "**Mining Your Database:** *Making More Sales Through People You Already Know*," you'll be doing considerably more than the average salesperson and definitely going beyond the obvious.

However, to really gain the advantage in your marketplace, begin using the techniques for meeting and working with strangers that I've given you in these pages. Few other salespeople and sales organizations in your market will come close to the type of lead generation you'll be capable of producing.

Reaching out to total strangers and strategically contacting other people in your marketplace that can help you in your business are ways that you can be intentional and proactive about expanding your business.

Intentionally Going After Success

Making the decision that you want to have more traffic or more people to talk with than you're getting now through traditional or conventional sources — and that you want it on a more consistent basis — is the first step to becoming a great traffic generator.

It is a conscious decision, and it requires willpower and commitment.

No one reaches this intentional decision without the earnest desire to act on it — unless it is just wishful thinking.

Wanting more traffic — as in it sure would be nice to have — is entirely different than doing something to actually make it happen.

This works in all market conditions — very competitive markets to very stubborn ones.

As long as there you have a product or service to sell and people to buy it, the techniques and strategies of traffic generation that I've discussed will work for you.

What better way to really go after potential customers than to begin meeting people that are not currently part of your circle of contacts?

The Power Of Strangers

The reason I've created this book for you that focuses on attracting and working with strangers is that they are limitless.

We are always meeting new people.

We can intentionally insert ourselves into a situation where there will be new people around us for us to make the initial contact. We just have to be where there is an opportunity to meet and engage people that we may not already know.

If we stay in our offices all day, go straight home when we leave the office, and hang around the house most of the time when we aren't at the office, we are going to have very limited opportunities to meet additional people.

Working with people we already know is great — that's an important component of generating our own leads.

However, working with strangers — and intentionally seeking them — is a concept few salespeople ever grasp.

You're In Charge Now

The amount of traffic or sales leads you can produce is limited only by your initiative and the amount of time devoted to it.

You have been given several scenarios in this book as ways to reach out to meet people not currently among your circle of contacts — in person, over the telephone, and through written correspondence.

Expand from there. This is a good start, but it is not intended to be exhaustive.

Begin thinking of even more ways that you can be around people that you may not know so that you can say hello to them and begin developing the contact.

Not every casual contact will develop into a sales lead or referral. Some people will stop you at just the initial contact, but others will allow you to call them.

Act as if the only people that you're going to get to make a presentation to are what you produce for yourself. This is the real key to your success.

You have to own your customer base — not necessarily in a legal sense but in a responsibility one. You have to continually add to it so it doesn't get stale. Own the creation of additional leads.

Your paradigm needs to be that you're in charge of producing the people that you meet with to create sales.

Anything else that comes your way through traditional or conventional advertising and marketing produced by you or your company, and incidental referrals from people you've already met in your sales center, showroom, or office, will just be a bonus.

Steve Hoffacker

Steve Hoffacker, AICP, CAASH, CAPS, CGA, CGP, CMP, CSP, MCSP, MIRM, is principal of Hoffacker Associates LLC, a West Palm Beach, Florida based real estate and small business sales and marketing consultancy and commercial real estate brokerage.

Steve is a sales trainer and coach, marketing consultant, photographer, commercial real estate broker, podcaster, blogger, teacher, author, writer, salesman, mentor, and motivational speaker.

For 30 years, he has helped homebuilders, salespeople (B2B and B2C), contractors, Realtors®, business owners, and entrepreneurs to be more visible, competitive, profitable, and effective — and to really enjoy what they are doing.

One of the keys to increased production and profitability is Steve's innovative customer connection program of intentional lead generation, customer rating, social networking, and post-visit contact that lets you reach out to potential customers, attract new leads, identify those people who are ready to make a decision, and maintain appropriate contact with others who need more time.

As a result, you will be making sales that otherwise might not have happened, and you can eliminate unnecessary expenditures of time, money, and energy in the process.